New Longman Shakespeare

Twelfth Night

William Shakespeare

edited by John O'Connor

 LONGMAN

Pearson Education Limited
Edinburgh Gate
Harlow
Essex
CM20 2JE
England and Associated Companies throughout the World

ISBN 0 582 36578 3

First published 1999
Fifth impression 2002
Printed in Singapore (FOP.)

The Publisher's policy is to use paper manufactured from
sustainable forests.

Acknowledgements

We are grateful to the following for permission to reproduce
photographs:

Donald Cooper/Photostage pages 76, 112 above and below
left, 158; Courtesy Entertainment releasing The Ronald Grant
Archive pages 128, 182; Zoe Dominic pages 89, 112 below
right; Mark Douet/The Royal Shakespeare Company page 52;
Mary Evans Picture Library/Ultrecht University Library page
208; Paul Mulcahy page 92; The Shakespeare Centre Library,
Stratford-upon-Avon pages 58, 88, 126; John Tramper page
209.

Cover Courtesy Entertainment releasing The Ronald Grant
Archive

Contents

Introduction

To the student

Shakespeare wrote *Twelfth Night* so that it could be performed by actors and enjoyed by audiences. To help you get the most out of the play, this edition includes:
- a complete **script**;
- **notes** printed next to the script which explain difficulties and point out important features;
- **activities** on the same page which will help you to focus on the scene you are reading;
- page-by-page **summaries** of the plot;
- **exam questions** after each Act, which will give you practice at the right level;
- **background information** about *Twelfth Night*, Shakespeare's theatre and the verse he uses; and
- **advice** on how to set out titles and quotations in your essays.

To the teacher

New Longman Shakespeare has been designed to meet the varied and complex needs of students working throughout the 11–16 age-range.

The textual notes

These have been newly written to provide understandable explanations which are easily located on the page:
- notes are placed next to the text with clear line references
- explanations of more complex words are given in context and help is provided with key imagery and historical references.

The activities

1 **Activities accompanying the text**

These are based on the premise that the text is best enjoyed and understood as a script for performance:

- In addition to a wide variety of reading, writing, listening and speaking activities, students are encouraged to: improvise, learn the script for performance, freeze-frame, rehearse, hot-seat, devise graphs and charts and create various forms of artwork, including storyboards, collages and cartoons.
- To provide a clear structure, activities are placed opposite the section of text to which they refer and come under five headings:
    - **i Character reviews** help students to think about the many different aspects of a given character which are presented in the course of the play. There might be as many as twenty of these activities on a single major character.
    - **ii Actors' interpretations** draw upon actual performances and ask students to consider comments from actors and directors in film and stage productions.
    - **iii Shakespeare's Language** activities, focusing on everything from imagery to word-play, enable students to understand how the dramatist's language works to convey the central ideas of the play.
    - **iv Plot reviews** help students to keep in mind the essential details of what is happening in the story as well as asking them to consider how the plot is structured.
    - **v Themes** are explored according to their predominance in each play.
- 'Serial activities' (Viola 1, . . . 2, . . . 3, for example) enable students to focus in detail on a single key features.

In addition, students who find extended tasks on Shakespeare a daunting prospect can combine several of these more focused activities – each in itself free-standing – to form the basis of a fuller piece of work.

2 Exam-style activities

At the end of each act – and also at the end of the book – there are activities which require SATs and GCSE style responses and offer opportunities for assessment.

3 Summative activities

Thinking about the play as a whole . . . is a section which offers a wide range of summative activities suitable for all levels.

Differentiation
Many students using this edition will be approaching Shakespeare for the first time; some might be studying the play for their Key Stage 3 SATs exam; others will be working towards GCSE.

Introduction

To answer their very different needs and interests, many of the activities
have been differentiated to match the National Curriculum Level
Descriptions and GCSE criteria. Activities of this kind are presented in three
levels:

A Foundation level activities, which support an initial reading of the play
and help students to build a solid basic knowledge and understanding.
B Activities geared towards the needs of Year 9 Key Stage 3 students
preparing for SATs.
C More advanced activities in line with GCSE requirements.

Plot summaries

As students work through the play, their understanding of the play's plot is
supported by:
• a brief headline summary at the top of each spread
• regular Plot Review activities
• a final detailed summary, scene by scene.

Background

Detailed fact-sheets are provided on:
• Shakespeare's England
• Plays and Playhouses
• The Globe Theatre
• The Social and Historical Background (to each particular play)
• Shakespeare's Life and his Times

Studying and writing about the play

To help students who are studying the play for examinations, there are
sections on:
• Shakespeare's verse (with examples from the particular play)
• Study Skills: Titles and Quotations

Characters in the play

Shipwrecked on the shores of Illyria:
VIOLA, a young woman who later disguises herself as a young man
called Cesario
The CAPTAIN of the ship
some sailors

Shipwrecked further along the coast:
SEBASTIAN, Viola's twin brother
ANTONIO, another sea captain who befriends Sebastian

In a palace in Illyria:
ORSINO, Duke of Illyria
VALENTINE and CURIO, gentlemen attending on him
other lords, officers and musicians

In a country house nearby:
OLIVIA, a rich Countess, whose father and brother have just died
MARIA, her waiting-gentlewoman
SIR TOBY BELCH, her uncle
SIR ANDREW AGUECHEEK, a visitor invited to the house by
Sir Toby
MALVOLIO, Olivia's steward
FABIAN, a member of the household
FESTE, the household fool or jester
A PRIEST
servants

All the scenes are set in Illyria, apart from 2.1, which takes place
further up the coast. Although Illyria actually exists (it is on the
Adriatic coast), Shakespeare's characters seem to inhabit a country
which, from most of the references in the play, is very like his own
England.

1.1 The Duke's palace, Illyria

Duke Orsino calls for music to feed his hunger for the love of the Countess Olivia.

Activities

Themes (1): love

As you read, watch or perform the play, look out for the many times that different characters talk about, or actually experience, love.

A In the very first line of the play, Orsino links love with music. As a class, make a list of song titles, or lines from songs, which include the word 'love'. When you get to the end of scene 2, see how many of them fit the situations or moods that Orsino and Viola are in, and create posters which use quotations from the play, lines from the songs and images taken from magazines.

B Think about the many different ways in which 'love' appears in magazines, novels, films and TV soaps – even advertisements. As a class, (a) list some of them; (b) discuss the particular difficulties that the lovers have experienced; and (c) decide whether any of those lovers behave in any way like Orsino at the beginning of this scene.

C In the course of studying this play, you will be focusing on five themes: Love; Appearance and Reality; Time; Fate; and Madness. Start a Theme Database, in which you simply note down line references as you encounter them, under each heading.

1–3 If music ... *Orsino thinks of music as being the 'food' that his love feeds on and he hopes that, if he has too much* (**excess**), *his love will die through overeating* (**surfeiting**).

4 the tune (**strain**) faded away at the end (**had a dying fall**)

9 quick and fresh lively and keen

12 Of what validity ... however excellent

13 falls into abatement ... loses its value

14–15 so full of shapes ... love is the most imaginative thing

16 hart deer. *(Orsino plays on the word: he hunts Olivia's 'heart'.)*

19 Olivia cleansed or purified (**purged**) the air of infection (**pestilence**).

20 That instant ... *In Greek mythology, Actaeon was turned into a deer by the goddess Diana and hunted to death.*

21 And my desires ... His love is like a deadly (**fell**) pack of hounds, chasing him.

25–31 Because she is in mourning for her brother, Olivia will not reveal her face to the air (**element**) for seven years, but will live like a nun (**cloistress**) and weep each day.

29 eye-offending brine salt tears, water that stings the eyes

29 season keep fresh (with salt)

Act 1

Scene 1

A room in the Duke's palace.

Enter DUKE, CURIO, lords; musicians attending.

DUKE	If music be the food of love, play on; *excess love*

DUKE If music be the food of love, play on; ⟩ *excess love*
Give me excess of it, that, surfeiting, ⟋
The appetite may sicken, and so die. —
That strain again! it had a dying fall;
O, it came o'er my ear like the sweet sound   5
That breathes upon a bank of violets,
Stealing and giving odour. Enough! no more;
'T is not so sweet now as it was before.
O spirit of love! how quick and fresh art thou,
That, notwithstanding thy capacity   10
Receiveth as the sea, nought enters there,
Of what validity and pitch soe'er,
But falls into abatement and low price,
Even in a minute; so full of shapes is fancy
That it alone is high fantastical.   15

CURIO Will you go hunt, my lord?

DUKE   What, Curio?

CURIO   The hart.

DUKE Why, so I do, the noblest that I have.
O, when mine eyes did see Olivia first,
Methought she purged the air of pestilence;
That instant was I turned into a hart,   20
And my desires, like fell and cruel hounds,
E'er since pursue me.

Enter VALENTINE.

(*To* VALENTINE) How now! What news from her?

VALENTINE So please my lord, I might not be admitted;
But from her handmaid do return this answer:
The element itself, till seven years' heat,   25
Shall not behold her face at ample view;
But, like a cloistress, she will veiléd walk,
And water once a day her chamber round
With eye-offending brine; all this to season

3

1.2 The sea-coast of Illyria

Viola and some sailors are washed up on the shore of Illyria after a shipwreck.

Activities

Character review: Olivia (1)

1. In pairs, re-read Valentine's speech ('The element itself . . . sad remembrance' – lines 25–31), picking out what you consider to be the key words or phrases in each line (such as 'seven years', 'face', 'cloistress' . . .).

2. Then perform the speech, emphasising those key words.

3. Imagine that Olivia's message, delivered by Valentine, had been written as a letter to Orsino. Write the letter, beginning 'My noble Duke Orsino . . .', explaining exactly why she will not listen to offers of love. Use your own words, but make sure that the language is appropriate for Olivia, and picks up the tone and meaning of the key words that you selected.

32–36 **O, she . . .** *Orsino feels that someone who can love a brother so deeply will surely love another man even more strongly.*

32 **frame** quality

34 **the rich golden shaft** the arrows of Cupid, god of love

35 **the flock . . .** all the other loves within her

36–38 **when liver . . .** when every perfect part of her is ruled by one person. *(In Shakespeare's time people believed that different emotions came from various organs of the body.)*

40 **Love thoughts . . .** The romantic Orsino can think of love best when lying under a flowery shelter.

1–3 **What country . . .** *Viola finds herself in Illyria, but fears that her brother is drowned and in* **Elysium** *(the mythological home of the dead).*

4 **Perchance** by chance, perhaps

7 **to comfort you . . .** *The Captain is trying to cheer Viola up with what might have happened.*

10 **driving** driven by the wind

11 **provident in peril** Her brother behaved intelligently in danger.

A brother's dead love, which she would keep
    fresh   30
And lasting in her sad remembrance.

DUKE   O, she that hath a heart of that fine frame
To pay this debt of love but to a brother,
How will she love, when the rich golden shaft
Hath killed the flock of all affections else   35
That live in her; when liver, brain, and heart,
These sovereign thrones, are all supplied, and filled
Her sweet perfections, with one self king!
Away before me to sweet beds of flowers;
Love-thoughts lie rich when canopied with
    bowers.   40

Exeunt.

Scene 2

The sea-coast.

Enter VIOLA, CAPTAIN and sailors.

VIOLA   What country, friends, is this?

CAPTAIN   This is Illyria, lady.

VIOLA   And what should I do in Illyria?
My brother he is in Elysium.
Perchance he is not drowned; what think you,
    sailors?

CAPTAIN   It is perchance that you yourself were saved.   5

VIOLA   O, my poor brother! and so perchance may he be.

CAPTAIN   True, madam; and, to comfort you with chance,
Assure yourself, after our ship did split,
When you and those poor number saved with
    you
Hung on our driving boat, I saw your brother,   10
Most provident in peril, bind himself –

5

1.2 The sea-coast of Illyria

The Captain explains that the country is ruled by a noble Duke called Orsino, a man Viola has heard of, who loves Countess Olivia.

Activities

Actors' interpretations (1): Viola's entrance

A In pairs, try to think up all the reasons a young woman, shipwrecked on a foreign shore, would have for feeling in danger. What other practical concerns would someone in her situation have?

B In preparation for a future written assignment on Viola, jot down quotations from this scene which illustrate Viola's strength of character (qualities such as resourcefulness, determination, courage, perceptiveness, practicality and optimism).

C When Helen Schlesinger played Viola in 1997, the scene opened with her in a hospital bed, tended by doctors and nurses. Discuss ways in which you can stage the opening of this scene, in order to give the audience a picture of a young woman who has just survived a shipwreck and is now exceedingly vulnerable. Choose one and either improvise it, or perform it using the script. As a class, discuss the different results.

12 **both teaching him** His courage and his hopes of survival both showed him what to do.

14 *In Greek mythology,* **Arion** *was saved from drowning by a dolphin.*

15 **hold acquaintance with ...** He 'stayed on good terms' with the waves.

17–19 **Mine own escape ...** The fact that I have escaped, plus what you have told me, helps me to believe that he might have escaped too.

28 **very late** recently

29 **for but a month ...** I left here only a month ago.

30 **'t was fresh in murmur** everybody was passing the rumour around

31 **What great ones do ...** Ordinary people always gossip about the nobility.

36 **In the protection of ...** *After the death of Olivia's father, her brother became her guardian, but he himself died shortly afterwards.*

38 **she hath abjured** For love of her dead brother, she has refused to be in men's company.

39–42 **O that I served ...** *Viola immediately gets the idea of working as one of Olivia's servants, and keeping her identity secret* (**not be delivered ...**) *until the time is ripe to reveal who she really is.*

Courage and hope both teaching him the practice –
To a strong mast that lived upon the sea;
Where, like Arion on the dolphin's back,
I saw him hold acquaintance with the waves   15
So long as I could see.

VIOLA   (*Giving him money*)   For saying so, there's gold;
Mine own escape unfoldeth to my hope,
Whereto thy speech serves for authority,
The like of him. Know'st thou this country?

CAPTAIN   Ay, madam, well; for I was bred and born   20
Not three hours' travel from this very place.

VIOLA   Who governs here?

CAPTAIN   A noble duke, in nature as in name.

VIOLA   What is his name?

CAPTAIN   Orsino.   25

VIOLA   Orsino! I have heard my father name him;
He was a bachelor then.

CAPTAIN   And so is now, or was so very late;
For but a month ago I went from hence,
And then 't was fresh in murmur – as, you know,   30
What great ones do the less will prattle of –
That he did seek the love of fair Olivia.

VIOLA   What's she?

CAPTAIN   A virtuous maid, the daughter of a count
That died some twelvemonth since; then leaving
          her   35
In the protection of his son, her brother,
Who shortly also died; for whose dear love,
They say, she hath abjured the company
And sight of men.

VIOLA   O that I served that lady,
And might not be delivered to the world   40
Till I had made mine own occasion mellow,
What my estate is!

7

1.3 A room in Olivia's house

Maria warns Sir Toby that Olivia is becoming irritated by his drinking and unruly behaviour.

42–44 That would be a difficult thing to achieve (**hard to compass**) because she won't accept any requests (**no kind of suit**), not even the duke's.

46–49 **And though ... character** Although badness (**pollution**) is often enclosed in an attractive outside (**beauteous wall**), I am prepared to believe you have a character (**mind**) which matches your pleasant appearance.

51 **Conceal me what I am** Keep my true identity secret.

51–53 And help me with whatever disguise might happen to be necessary for (**haply shall become**) my plans (**my intent**).

57 **That will allow me ...** That will prove that I am worth employing.

59 **Only shape thou ...** Keep quiet about my clever plan.

61 **When my tongue ...** If I blab, put out my eyes!

4 **By my troth** Honestly

5 **cousin** *In Shakespeare's time 'cousin' could be used for any close relative.*

5–6 Olivia objects strongly (**takes great exceptions**) to her uncle's late nights (**ill hours**).

7 **let her except ...** *A lawyer's phrase:* 'If she's excused my behaviour before, she can excuse it again!'

1.3

CAPTAIN	That were hard to compass,
	Because she will admit no kind of suit,
	No, not the duke's.

VIOLA There is a fair behaviour in thee, captain; 45
And though that nature with a beauteous wall
Doth oft close in pollution, yet of thee
I will believe thou hast a mind that suits
With this thy fair and outward character,
I prithee – and I'll pay thee bounteously – 50
Conceal me what I am, and be my aid
For such disguise as haply shall become
The form of my intent. I'll serve this duke;
Thou shalt present me as an eunuch to him;
It may be worth thy pains; for I can sing 55
And speak to him in many sorts of music
That will allow me very worth his service.
What else may hap, to time I will commit;
Only shape thou thy silence to my wit.

CAPTAIN Be you his eunuch, and your mute I'll be; 60
When my tongue blabs, then let mine eyes not see.

VIOLA I thank thee; lead me on.

Exeunt.

Scene 3

A room in Olivia's house.

Enter SIR TOBY BELCH and MARIA.

SIR TOBY What a plague means my niece, to take the death
of her brother thus? I am sure care's an enemy to
life.

MARIA By my troth, Sir Toby, you must come in earlier
o' nights; your cousin, my lady, takes great 5
exceptions to your ill hours.

SIR TOBY Why, let her except before excepted.

1.3 A room in Olivia's house

Sir Toby and Maria discuss the foolish Sir Andrew Aguecheek, whom
Sir Toby has invited to the house to woo Olivia.

Activities

Shakespeare's language: (1) language and character

Many of the characters in this play (and other Shakespeare plays) love playing with words, especially where they have double meanings. (Do you recall Orsino's play on the word 'hart'? Look back at 1.1.16–22.)

A When Mercutio in *Romeo and Juliet* realises that he has been fatally wounded, he says, 'Ask for me tomorrow and you shall find me a grave man.'

1. Discuss that example of wordplay, making sure that you understand how the speaker has used the two meanings of the word 'grave'.

2. Can you think of other jokes involving wordplay which depends on double meanings (sometimes known as 'puns')?

Discuss the following examples,
B checking that you understand the double meanings:

• 8–10: When Maria tells Sir Toby that he must confine himself, she means 'restrain; keep within the rules of reasonable behaviour'. But 'confine' can also mean 'dress', so he says that he will dress as he likes: 'I'll confine myself no finer'.

(Continued on page 12)

8–9 you must confine . . . You must keep within the rules of reasonable behaviour.

10 I'll confine myself . . . *'Confine' can also mean 'dress up'. Sir Toby refuses to put on any smarter clothes than the ones he is wearing.*

12 an if

14 quaffing draining a glass all in one go

14 undo you be the ruin of you

22 ducats gold coins. *Aguecheek is quite wealthy.*

23–24 Ay, but he'll have . . . Yes, but it will only take him one year to get through all those ducats; he's a complete (**very**) fool and a waster (**prodigal**).

25 Fie Nonsense!

25–26 viol-de-gamboys *a musical instrument something like a cello*

27 without book by heart *(perhaps parrot-fashion, without understanding a word!)*

29 almost natural *Idiots were often called 'naturals'.*

30–33 but that he hath . . . If he didn't have such a talent for cowardice, to reduce (**allay**) his enthusiasm (**gust**) for quarrelling, wise people (**the prudent**) say he would soon be dead.

34 substractors *Toby invents this word to mean 'slanderers'. Maria plays on the words 'subtract' and 'add' in line 36.*

MARIA	Ay, but you must confine yourself within the modest limits of order.
SIR TOBY	Confine! I'll confine myself no finer than I am. These clothes are good enough to drink in, and so be these boots too; an they be not, let them hang themselves in their own straps.
MARIA	That quaffing and drinking will undo you; I heard my lady talk of it yesterday; and of a foolish knight that you brought in one night here to be her wooer.
SIR TOBY	Who? Sir Andrew Aguecheek?
MARIA	Ay, he.
SIR TOBY	He's as tall a man as any's in Illyria.
MARIA	What's that to the purpose?
SIR TOBY	Why, he has three thousand ducats a year.
MARIA	Ay, but he'll have but a year in all these ducats; he's a very fool and a prodigal.
SIR TOBY	Fie, that you'll say so! He plays o' the viol-de-gamboys, and speaks three or four languages word for word without book, and hath all the good gifts of nature.
MARIA	He hath indeed, almost natural; for besides that he's a fool, he's a great quarreller; and but that he hath the gift of a coward to allay the gust he hath in quarrelling, 't is thought among the prudent he would quickly have the gift of a grave.
SIR TOBY	By this hand, they are scoundrels and substractors that say so of him. Who are they?
MARIA	They that add, moreover, he's drunk nightly in your company.
SIR TOBY	With drinking healths to my niece. I'll drink to her as long as there is a passage in my throat and

10

15

20

25

30

35

1.3 A room in Olivia's house

Sir Andrew Aguecheek enters and shows how stupid he is.

Activities

- 20–21: tall . . . Toby means 'important and well known', but Maria asks what his height has got to do with it.
- 25–26: The viol-de-gamboys was held between the knees, so this is a sexual joke.
- 27–33: Sir Toby says that Aguecheek has 'all the good gifts of nature'; Maria picks up the word natural, meaning a born fool, and also plays with the word 'gifts'.
- 34–36: Toby calls the people who criticise Aguecheek substractors; Maria says that the same people add that he's always drunk.

Discuss what this frequent wordplay seems to reveal about the kinds of people Sir Toby and Maria are, and the relationship between them.

C As preparation for an essay on 'Shakespeare's wordplay in *Twelfth Night*', start a list of examples of wordplay and add to it, creating a wordplay database as you go through the play. Note the way the wordplay works in each case and try to say why the speaker is engaging in it (for example: to give a clever reply; to insult someone; to baffle them; simply for the love of playing with words . . .), and what it reveals about the character or their relationship with another character.

40 **coystril** villain

42 **parish-top** *Villages kept large spinning-tops for people to exercise with.*

42–43 ***Castiliano vulgo!*** *This sounds Spanish (and possibly rude), but nobody knows what it means.*

43 **Agueface** *Sir Toby mocks Aguecheek's name, perhaps because he looks gloomy.*

46 **fair shrew** *Sir Andrew is probably trying to be polite, since shrews are sweet little creatures. Unfortunately, the word meant a bad-tempered woman!*

48 **Accost** Go up and greet her politely.

51 *Not understanding the meaning of 'Accost', Sir Andrew thinks it is her name.*

55–56 **front her, board her** . . . *These are all words to describe a rather violent approach to sex. Sir Andrew is understandably embarrassed.*

57 **undertake her** 'tackle' her

60 **An thou let part so** if you let her leave you like this

64 **. . . fools in hand?** Do you think you're dealing with idiots?

66 **Marry** By the Virgin Mary! (*a very mild swear word*)

drink in Illyria. He's a coward and a coystril that 40
will nor drink to my niece till his brains turn o'
the toe like a parish-top. What, wench! *Castiliano*
vulgo! for here comes Sir Andrew Agueface.

Enter SIR ANDREW AGUECHEEK.

SIR ANDREW Sir Toby Belch! How now, Sir Toby Belch!

SIR TOBY Sweet Sir Andrew! 45

SIR ANDREW (*To* MARIA) Bless you, fair shrew.

MARIA And you too, sir.

SIR TOBY Accost, Sir Andrew, accost.

SIR ANDREW What's that?

SIR TOBY My niece's chambermaid. 50

SIR ANDREW Good Mistress Accost, I desire better
acquaintance.

MARIA My name is Mary, sir.

SIR ANDREW Good Mistress Mary Accost –

SIR TOBY You mistake, knight; "accost" is front her, board 55
her, woo her, assail her.

SIR ANDREW By my troth, I would not undertake her in this
company. Is that the meaning of "accost"?

MARIA Fare you well, gentlemen.

SIR TOBY An thou let part so, Sir Andrew, would thou 60
might'st never draw sword again!

SIR ANDREW An you part so, mistress, I would I might never
draw sword again. Fair lady, do you think you
have fools in hand?

MARIA Sir, I have not you by the hand. 65

SIR ANDREW Marry, but you shall have; and here's my hand.

1.3 A room in Olivia's house

Maria completes her mockery of Sir Andrew and leaves him feeling dejected.

Activities

Character review: Maria (1)

In pairs, re-read lines 44–76, in which Sir Andrew meets Maria, and note down all the clues that the dialogue gives you about how the characters should move and what actions they should do. (For example, Sir Andrew has to go up to Maria and at another point she takes his hand.)

1. Act out the episode, bringing out:
   - Sir Andrew's awkwardness with Maria
   - his misunderstanding of the word 'accost'
   - Maria's cleverness in 'putting him down'.
2. Discuss what this episode reveals about the kind of person Maria is, in your opinion. Do you, for example, find her mocking of Sir Andrew cruel? Or do you simply admire her cleverness?

68 **buttery-bar** a ledge for resting drink on outside the liquor store.

69 **What's your metaphor?** What's your hidden meaning?

70 **dry** (1) thirsty; (2) It was believed that people with a dry palm were sexually impotent.

73 **A dry jest** an ironical joke

75–76 **at my fingers' ends ...** *(1) always ready and 'to hand'; (2) she is holding Sir Andrew's hand so he is the joke. When she lets his hand go, she is* **barren:** *(1) she no longer has any jokes; (2) she no longer has hold of a fool.*

77 **thou lackest ...** You need a drink! *(Canary was wine from the Canary Islands.)*

78 **put down** defeated *(in lines 79–80 Sir Andrew then thinks of the other meaning: falling down drunk)*

82 **beef** *People thought that they would become stupid if they ate too much 'heavy' meat.*

85 **forswear it** give it up

87–88 ***Pourquoi*** *Sir Toby asks 'Why?' in French, but Sir Andrew does not understand.*

89 **the tongues** foreign languages

92–97 *Sir Toby puns on 'tongues' and 'tongs' – which would have helped Sir Andrew's straight hair to curl.*

14

MARIA	Now, sir, "thought is free"; I pray you, bring your hand to the buttery-bar and let it drink.
SIR ANDREW	Wherefore, sweetheart? What's your metaphor?
MARIA	It's dry, sir.
SIR ANDREW	Why, I think so; I am not such an ass but I can keep my hand dry. But what's your jest?
MARIA	A dry jest, sir.
SIR ANDREW	Are you full of them?
MARIA	Ay, sir, I have them at my fingers' ends; marry, now I let go your hand, I am barren.

Exit.

SIR TOBY	O knight! thou lackest a cup of canary; when did I see thee so put down?
SIR ANDREW	Never in your life, I think; unless you see canary put me down. Methinks sometimes I have no more wit than a Christian or an ordinary man has; but I am a great eater of beef, and I believe that does harm to my wit.
SIR TOBY	No question.
SIR ANDREW	An I thought that, I'd forswear it. I'll ride home tomorrow, Sir Toby.
SIR TOBY	*Pourquoi*, my dear knight?
SIR ANDREW	What is "*pourquoi*"? Do or not do? I would I had bestowed that time in the tongues that I have in fencing, dancing, and bear-baiting. O! had I but followed the arts!
SIR TOBY	Then hadst thou had an excellent head of hair.
SIR ANDREW	Why, would that have mended my hair?
SIR TOBY	Past question; for thou seest it will not curl by nature.

70

75

80

85

90

95

1.3 A room in Olivia's house

Sir Andrew performs some dance steps for Sir Toby, who tells him what a brilliant mover he is.

Activities

Character review: Sir Andrew (1)

A Recap on what exactly Sir Andrew is doing in Olivia's house. Who has invited him? What are his hopes?

B Discuss what image you think Sir Andrew has of himself. Look back at:
- the things he says about himself
- the ways in which he responds to other people's comments. Write Sir Andrew's diary entry for that day, in which he records his meeting with Maria and dancing for Sir Toby. Try to write in an appropriate style (but using standardised spelling!), and make sure that the letter conveys an impression of Sir Andrew's image of himself, as well as of other characters.

C Look back through the scene and note down the moments which reveal that Sir Andrew frequently misses the point and is not very bright, explaining exactly what happens in each case. (For example, look at his reaction to 'accost' and 'Pourquoi?', and his treatment at Maria's hands.)

97 **like flax on a distaff** *Flax is a pale yellow fibre, wound on to a stick for spinning.*

97–99 **I hope to see ...** *(1) A housewife might treat the skinny Sir Andrew as a distaff and spin off his flax-like hair; (2) a prostitute might have sex with him and give him syphilis which would make his hair fall out.*

104–105 **she'll not match ...** She won't marry anyone superior, either in social rank (**estate**), age or intelligence.

110 **kickshawses** (French 'quelquechose') 'little somethings' such as fancy dance steps

111–112 **under the degree ...** so long as they're not above me in social class

114 **What is thy excellence ... ?** How good are you at a galliard? *(an energetic dance)*

115 **cut a caper** jump high in the air *(in line 116 Toby puns on the spice 'caper', which goes with mutton)*

117 **back-trick** a backwards leap

121 **Mistress Mall** *Nobody really knows who she was.*

123 **coranto** a running dance

124–125 **I would not so much ...** If I had your talent, I wouldn't even urinate without dancing!

124–125 **sink-a-pace** a five-step dance

SIR ANDREW But it becomes me well enough, does it not?

SIR TOBY Excellent; it hangs like flax on a distaff, and I
hope to see a housewife take thee between her
legs, and spin it off.

SIR ANDREW Faith, I'll home tomorrow, Sir Toby; your niece   100
will not be seen; or if she be, it's four to one she'll
none of me. The count himself here hard by woos
her.

SIR TOBY She'll none o' the count; she'll not match above
her degree, neither in estate, years, nor wit; I have   105
heard swear it. Tut, there's life in 't, man.

SIR ANDREW I'll stay a month longer. I am a fellow o' the
strangest mind i' the world; I delight in masques
and revels sometimes altogether.

SIR TOBY Art thou good at these kickshawses, knight?   110

SIR ANDREW As any man in Illyria, whatsoever he be, under the
degree of my betters; and yet I will not compare
with an old man.

SIR TOBY What is thy excellence in a galliard, knight?

SIR ANDREW Faith, I can cut a caper.   115

SIR TOBY And I can cut the mutton to 't.

SIR ANDREW And I think I have the back-trick simply as strong
as any man in Illyria.

He dances.

SIR TOBY Wherefore are these things hid? Wherefore have
these gifts a curtain before 'em? Are they like to   120
take dust, like Mistress Mall's picture? Why dost
thou not go to church in a galliard, and come
home in a coranto? My very walk should be a jig;
I would not so much as make water but in a sink-
a-pace. What dost thou mean? Is it a world to   125
hide virtues in? I did think, by the excellent
constitution of thy leg, it was formed under the
star of a galliard.

1.4 The Duke's palace

In her disguise as a young man called Cesario, Viola has already made a good impression.

Activities

Character review: Sir Toby (1)

What early impressions have you formed of Sir Toby? What do we learn about the way he lives, his attitudes to others and the way others view him? Think about:

- his conversation with Maria, including his attitude to Olivia's mourning
- why you think he is so keen to keep Sir Andrew in the house
- the way he persuades Sir Andrew to stay.

Do you find him an attractive character, on first appearance?

Character review: Orsino (1)

Orsino says to Cesario: 'I have unclasped To thee the book even of my secret soul.' Write in your own words what Orsino might have said, in telling Cesario everything about his love for Olivia. As preparation, (a) re-read what he says in scene 1; and (b) discuss what the relationship seems to be with Cesario.

---

129 **it does indifferent well** it looks pretty good

130 **stock** stockings

134–135 **Taurus ...** *People thought that each section of the body was controlled by a particular sign of the zodiac.*

2 **Cesario** *This is the name that Viola has adopted in her disguise as a young man.*

2 **like to be much advanced** likely to get a very good job here

3 **but three days** *Notice how Shakespeare lets us know that time has passed.*

5 **fear his humour or my negligence** You're either worried that he might change his mind or that I will stop serving him properly.

7 **inconstant** unreliable

11 **On your attendance** I am here to wait upon you.

12 **aloof** at a distance

13 **Thou know'st ...** You know absolutely everything. *(In only three days, Orsino has become so impressed by 'Cesario' that he has revealed everything about his love for Olivia.)*

13 **unclasped** opened

SIR ANDREW	Ay, 't is strong, and it does indifferent well in a
	flame-coloured stock. Shall we set about some 130
	revels?

SIR TOBY	What shall we do else? Were we not born under
	Taurus?

SIR ANDREW	Taurus! that's sides and heart.

SIR TOBY	No, sir, it is legs and thighs. Let me see thee caper. 135
	(*SIR ANDREW dances again*) Ha! higher; ha, ha!
	excellent!

Exeunt.

Scene 4

A room in the Duke's palace.

Enter VALENTINE, and VIOLA in man's attire.

VALENTINE	If the duke continue these favours towards you,
	Cesario, you are like to be much advanced; he
	hath known you but three days and already you
	are no stranger.

VIOLA	(*who has taken the name CESARIO*)
	You either fear his humour or my negligence, that 5
	you call in question the continuance of his love.
	Is he inconstant, sir, in his favours?

VALENTINE	No, believe me.

VIOLA	I thank you. Here comes the count.

Enter DUKE, CURIO and attendants.

DUKE	Who saw Cesario, ho? 10

VIOLA	On your attendance, my lord; here.

DUKE	(*To the attendants*) Stand you awhile aloof. (*To VIOLA*)
	Cesario,
	Thou know'st no less but all; I have unclasped
	To thee the book even of my secret soul.

1.4 The Duke's palace

Given the job of carrying Orsino's love messages to Olivia, Viola realises that she has fallen in love with him herself.

Activities

Plot review (2): Viola's postcard

Write a postcard from Viola to the Sea Captain who helped her in the shipwreck, updating him on what has happened. Remember that messages on postcards (a) have to be brief; and (b) are not private. In other words, you cannot write much, and you have to be very careful about what you say.

Shakespeare's language (2): rhyming couplets

Shakespeare frequently concludes a scene with a rhyming couplet, as he does here: 'Yet, a barful strife! Whoe'er I woo, myself would be his wife.' Discuss what the rhyme seems to add to Viola's declaration of her love for Orsino. Does the rhyme make her statement sound sudden and impetuous? Silly? Determined?

15 **address thy gait** . . . direct your steps to her

21–22 **Be clamorous, and leap all civil bounds** . . . Make a fuss and break all the rules of polite behaviour, rather than return unsuccessfully.

25 **Surprise her with discourse** . . . overcome her with talk of my true love

27–28 **attend it better** pay more attention to it than through a messenger (**nuncio**) who was more serious looking (**of more grave aspect**)

30–31 **For they shall yet belie** . . . Anyone who calls you a 'man' is falsely describing your fortunate youthfulness.

31 **Diana** *was the virgin goddess. Her lips would have been smooth and ruby red* (**rubious**).

32–33 **thy small pipe** . . . Your high voice is like a girl's, shrill and unbroken (**sound**).

34 **all is semblative** . . . Everything about you looks feminine.

35–36 **thy constellation** . . . Your whole character

38–40 **Prosper well** . . . If you do well, you will have the same lifestyle as me, and share my wealth.

41 **a barful strife!** *Viola reveals that this is a difficult task* (**strife**) *full of obstacles* (**barful**): *whoever she woos on Orsino's behalf, she wants to marry him herself!*

Therefore, good youth, address thy gait unto her; 15
Be not denied access, stand at her doors,
And tell them, there thy fixéd foot shall grow
Till thou have audience.

VIOLA   Sure, my noble lord,
If she be so abandoned to her sorrow
As it is spoke, she never will admit me.   20

DUKE   Be clamorous, and leap all civil bounds,
Rather than make unprofited return.

VIOLA   Say I do speak with her, my lord; what then?

DUKE   O! then unfold the passion of my love;   ← *if he can't tell her how much he really love her?*
Surprise her with discourse of my dear faith;   25
It shall become thee well to act my woes;
She will attend it better in thy youth
Than in a nuncio's of more grave aspect.

VIOLA   I think not so, my lord.

DUKE   Dear lad, believe it;
For they shall yet belie thy happy years   30   *Blazon*
That say thou art a man; Diana's lip
Is not more smooth and rubious; thy small pipe
Is as the maiden's organ, shrill and sound,
Could be sexual? And all is semblative a woman's part.
I know thy constellation is right apt   35
For this affair. (*To the attendants*) Some four or five
      attend him –
All, if you will; for I myself am best
When least in company. Prosper well in this,
And thou shalt live as freely as thy lord,
To call his fortune thine.

VIOLA   I'll do my best   40
To woo your lady. (*Aside*) Yet, a barful strife!
Whoe'er I woo, myself would be his wife.

if a boy said this to a woman guy would they fake it rightly?

Thinking alloud

Exeunt.

reminder: she is a woman & is going to marry

21

1.5 Olivia's house

Maria warns Feste that he is in trouble for staying away from the house.

Activities

Character review: Feste (1)

A Read the section on fools on page 212 and discuss how successfully Feste seems to be doing his job in Olivia's household.

B It is sometimes possible to learn about a play's themes and characters by looking at the way a section of the script seems to feature a particular word class (such as nouns, adjectives or verbs). Abstract nouns play a major part in the opening 20 lines of dialogue between Feste and Maria.

1. Find the following abstract nouns in the script:
   excuse; absence; answer; foolery; wisdom; talents; a hanging; marriage; summer.
2. Why are the first five important for our understanding of the character of Feste and the situation he is in?

C Discuss what has been established about Feste from his first conversation with Maria. What is his status in the household? How would you describe his relationship with Maria? What is enigmatic about him?

2–3 **in way of thy excuse** in making excuses for you

5–6 **he that is well hanged ...** A dead man doesn't have to worry about the wars *(where 'colours' or military banners are flown).*

7 **Make that good** Explain the joke.

8 **He shall see none ...** If he's dead, he won't fear enemy colours.

9 **lenten** weak *(like boring food eaten in Lent)*

12 **that may you be bold to say** that would be a cheeky answer to give Olivia

14–15 **Well, God ...** *Feste often utters clever-sounding nonsense.*

19 **Many a good hanging ...** *He is suggesting that an unhappy marriage is a fate worse than death.*

20 **let summer bear it out** the warm weather will make it bearable

21 **resolute** determined

23–24 **That if one break ...** *Maria completes Feste's joke. He is punning on points in an argument and the laces (called 'points') which keep his trousers* **(gaskins)** *up.*

25 **very apt** very clever

25–27 **if Sir Toby ...** If you could get Sir Toby to give up drinking you would be the cleverest woman **(piece of Eve's flesh)** in Illyria.

Scene 5

A room in Olivia's house.

Enter MARIA and FESTE, the clown.

MARIA	Nay, either tell me where thou hast been, or I will not open my lips so wide as a bristle may enter in way of thy excuse. My lady will hang thee for thy absence.
FESTE	Let her hang me; he that is well hanged in this world needs to fear no colours. 5
MARIA	Make that good.
FESTE	He shall see none to fear.
MARIA	A good lenten answer; I can tell thee where that saying was born, of "I fear no colours". 10
FESTE	Where, good Mistress Mary?
MARIA	In the wars; and that may you be bold to say in your foolery.
FESTE	Well, God give them wisdom that have it; and those that are fools, let them use their talents. 15
MARIA	Yet you will be hanged for being so long absent; or, to be turned away, is not that as good as a hanging to you?
FESTE	Many a good hanging prevents a bad marriage; and, for turning away, let summer bear it out. 20
MARIA	You are resolute, then?
FESTE	Not so, neither; but I am resolved on two points.
MARIA	That if one break, the other will hold; or, if both break, your gaskins fall.
FESTE	Apt, in good faith; very apt. Well, go thy way; if 25 Sir Toby would leave drinking, thou wert as witty a piece of Eve's flesh as any in Ilyria.

Handwritten margin notes: ← someone could say this in any time)

Handwritten margin note: ← True

23

1.5 Olivia's house

Feste tries to use his wit to save himself from being taken away.

<table>
<tr><td valign="top">

Activities

Character review: Olivia (2)

We have heard things from other characters about Olivia, but this is the first time we see her, according to Shakespeare's script.

Look back at earlier scenes (and the activity on page 4) and jot down what we know about her already. What sort of woman is she? What feelings is she experiencing? What are her main concerns?

Then discuss how you would introduce her to the audience if you were directing the play.

1. How should she appear here? What should she be wearing, for example? (something expensive? a mourning costume?) How should she behave as she enters? (impatient? superior? dreamy? distracted? bad-tempered? unhappy?).

2. In some productions, Olivia is actually seen before this point, silently mourning at her brother's grave. Discuss the advantages and disadvantages of letting the audience receive an earlier view of her in this way.

</td><td valign="top">

30   **Wit . . .** *Feste asks his wit to help him come up with some good jokes.*

31–33   **Those wits that think . . .** People who think they're clever are often stupid; I know I'm stupid, but can convince people that I'm clever.

33–34   **Quinapalus** *Feste is pretending to quote some great scholar.*

39   **Go to** Go away

39   **dry** *Olivia means 'barren' – his jokes have dried up; in lines 41–43 Feste takes it to mean 'thirsty'.*

41   **madonna** my lady

45   **botcher** someone who mends clothes

47   **virtue that transgresses** goodness that does wrong

49   **syllogism** an argument using logic

50–51   **As there is no true cuckold . . .** *This is deliberately difficult, but the general meaning is: 'As your grief for your brother will not last, get married before your beauty fades.'*

55   **Misprision . . .** misunderstanding of the very worst sort

55–56   **cucullus . . .** *A Latin proverb: 'Just because someone wears a hood, that doesn't make him a monk.' ('I might dress like a fool, but I'm not stupid!'.* **Motley** *is the fool's coloured outfit.*

</td></tr>
</table>

MARIA	Peace, you rogue, no more o' that. Here comes my lady; make your excuse wisely, you were best.

Exit.

FESTE	Wit, an 't be thy will, put me into good fooling! Those wits that think they have thee, do very oft prove fools; and I, that am sure I lack thee, may pass for a wise man; for what says Quinapalus? "Better a witty fool than a foolish wit."	30

Enter OLIVIA, MALVOLIO and attendants.

	God bless thee, lady!	35
OLIVIA	Take the fool away.	
FESTE	(*To the attendants*) Do you not hear, fellows? Take away the lady.	
OLIVIA	(*To FESTE*) Go to, you're a dry fool; I'll no more of you; besides, you grow dishonest.	40
FESTE	Two faults, madonna, that drink and good counsel will amend; for give the dry fool drink, then is the fool not dry; bid the dishonest man mend himself; if he mend, he is no longer dishonest; if he cannot, let the botcher mend him. Anything that's mended is but patched; virtue that transgresses is but patched with sin; and sin that amends is but patched with virtue. If that this simple syllogism will serve, so; if it will not, what remedy? As there is no true cuckold but calamity, so beauty's a flower. The lady bade take away the fool; therefore, I say again, take her away.	45

50 |
OLIVIA	Sir, I bade them take away *you*.	
FESTE	Misprision in the highest degree! Lady, *cucullus non facit monachum*: that's as much to say as I wear not motley in my brain. Good madonna, give me leave to prove you a fool.	55
OLIVIA	Can you do it?	

1.5 Olivia's house

Feste wittily proves Olivia a fool, but Malvolio is unimpressed and humiliates him.

Activities

Character review: Feste (2)

The way in which Feste manages to prove that Olivia is the fool who ought to be taken away is particularly clever. To see how his argument works, re-read the section in pairs (lines 57–72) and then act it out.

You can use whatever gestures or actions you think necessary, but you are allowed only one word from the script per sentence. Decide which are the key words, practise the dialogue, and then perform it, afterwards comparing your version with other people's.

60 **Dexteriously** very skilfully

62 **catechize** teach you by asking questions

63 **mouse** *an affectionate term (unlike Aguecheek's 'shrew')*

64–65 **for want of other idleness ...** Since I have nothing else to do, I'll wait for your argument.

74 **mend** improve, get funnier

76–77 **infirmity ...** The weakness of old age, which is harmful to wise people, always helps fools to improve.

78 **speedy infirmity** sudden illness

80 **no fox** *Foxes have always been known for their cleverness.*

84 **barren** unfunny, lacking in wit

85 **ordinary fool** a jester employed by an inn

86 **out of his guard** he has no answer

87–88 **unless ...** Unless you laugh and give him the opportunity to be funny (**minister occasion to him**), he is lost for words (**gagged**).

88–90 **I take ...** I consider sensible people who laugh uproariously (**crow**) at these fools who come out with rehearsed jokes (**these set kind ...**) to be no better than the fools' assistants (**zanies**).

91–92 **taste with a distempered appetite** *Malvolio cannot enjoy humour, just as sick people cannot enjoy food.*

| FESTE | Dexteriously, good madonna. | 60 |

| OLIVIA | Make your proof. |

| FESTE | I must catechize you for it, madonna; good my mouse of virtue, answer me. |

| OLIVIA | Well, sir, for want of other idleness, I'll bide your proof. | 65 |

| FESTE | Good madonna, why mournest thou? |

| OLIVIA | Good fool, for my brother's death. |

| FESTE | I think his soul is in hell, madonna. |

| OLIVIA | I know his soul is in heaven, fool. |

| FESTE | The more fool, madonna, to mourn for your brother's soul being in heaven. (*To the attendants*) Take away the fool, gentlemen. | 70 |

← why mourn that he is in a good place?

| OLIVIA | (*To MALVOLIO*) What think you of this fool, Malvolio? Doth he not mend? |

| MALVOLIO | Yes; and shall do till the pangs of death shake him; infirmity, that decays the wise, doth ever make the better fool. | 75 |

| FESTE | God send you, sir, a speedy infirmity, for the better increasing your folly! Sir Toby will be sworn that I am no fox, but he will not pass his word for two pence that you are no fool. | 80 |

| OLIVIA | How say you to that, Malvolio? |

| MALVOLIO | I marvel your ladyship takes delight in such a barren rascal; I saw him put down the other day with an ordinary fool that has no more brain than a stone. Look you now, he's out of his guard already; unless you laugh and minister occasion to him, he is gagged. I protest, I take these wise men, that crow so at these set kind of fools, no better than the fools' zanies. | 85 |
| | | 90 |

| OLIVIA | O, you are sick of self-love, Malvolio, and taste |

1.5 Olivia's house

Olivia stands up for Feste and for fools in general. Maria reports that there is a young visitor at the gate, and Sir Toby enters, drunk.

Activities

Actors' interpretations (2): Feste and Malvolio

Because Shakespeare did not include stage directions telling the actors what to do, they have the opportunity to make their own choices about how to react, but this can be especially difficult in the moments when they are not actually speaking.

Look again at lines 75–100 and (a) discuss which features of Malvolio's and Feste's characters are revealed; then (b) decide how Malvolio and Feste should react when they are not speaking. Make notes related to the script (for example, next to l.74 you might write: 'Looking pleased with himself.') and then rehearse the dialogue in line with your decisions.

Shakespeare's language (3): Names

Think about each of the following names:
Sir Toby Belch   Sir Andrew Aguecheek
Malvolio
All the words in these names have associations, which might hint at something about the character.

1. What do belch and ague mean and what might they suggest about the characters?
2. What does the prefix mal- usually denote?

92–95 **To be ...** People who are generous, innocent and good-natured don't take this kind of thing seriously. (**Bird-bolts** *were harmless flat-headed arrows.*)

95–98 **There is no slander ...** *Olivia points out to Malvolio that it is Feste's job to make fun of people (***rail***): they should not take offence. Similarly she tells Feste that sensible (***discreet***) people can criticise (***reprove***) somebody, without it being taken as an insult.*

99–100 **Mercury ...** May the god of cheating teach you to be a good liar – as you will have to be to speak well of fools!

108–109 **Fetch him off ...** Get him out of the way ... he talks like a madman.

110 **suit** request *(to do with love)*

114 **grows old** *Olivia implies that people have become tired of Feste's stale jokes.*

118 ***pia mater*** *Latin for the covering of the brain*

with a distempered appetite. To be generous,
guiltless, and of free disposition, is to take those
things for bird-bolts that you deem cannon-
bullets. There is no slander in an allowed fool, 　　95
though he do nothing but rail; nor no railing in a
known discreet man, though he do nothing but
reprove.

FESTE　　　Now, Mercury endue thee with leasing, for thou
speakest well of fools! 　　　　　　　　　　　　100

Re-enter MARIA.

MARIA　　　Madam, there is at the gate a young gentleman
much desires to speak with you.

OLIVIA　　From the count Orsino, is it?

MARIA　　　I know not, madam; 't is a fair young man, and
well attended. 　　　　　　　　　　　　　　105

OLIVIA　　Who of my people hold him in delay?

MARIA　　　Sir Toby, madam, your kinsman.

OLIVIA　　Fetch him off, I pray you; he speaks nothing but
madman. Fie on him!

Exit MARIA.

Go you, Malvolio; if it be a suit from the count, I 　110
am sick, or not at home, what you will, to dismiss
it.

Exit MALVOLIO.

(*To FESTE*) Now you see, sir, how your fooling
grows old, and people dislike it.

FESTE　　　Thou hast spoke for us, madonna, as if thy eldest 　115
son should be a fool; whose skull Jove cram with
brains! for here he comes, one of thy kin has a
most weak *pia mater*.

Enter SIR TOBY BELCH.

1.5 Olivia's house

Having given a drunken report of the visitor, Sir Toby leaves and Feste follows to look after him.

Activities

Themes (2): madness

When Olivia asks Feste: 'What's a drunken man like, fool?' he replies: 'Like a drowned man, a fool, and a madman; one draught above heat makes him a fool, the second mads him, and a third drowns him' (133–135); and he adds: 'He is but mad yet, madonna; and the fool shall look to the madman.'

As the play progresses, we are faced with questions such as 'What do we mean by mad?' 'What kinds of madness are there?' (Here, for example, madness is used to describe a state of drunkenness.) Start a list of the occasions in which characters refer to madness in this play, and keep a note of what they say about it.

119   **What** Who

123   **a plague ...** *Sir Toby has obviously belched at this point and blames the food!*

124   **How now, sot!** How's things, fool? *(Sot could also mean drunkard.)*

127–128   **lethargy ... lechery** *Olivia asks Sir Toby how he has come to be so 'sleepy' so early in the day; he thinks he is being accused of lustfulness (**lechery**).*

130–131   **Let him be the devil ...** He can be the devil if he wants, I don't care ... it makes no difference to me.

133–134   **one draught above heat** one drink too many *(that makes him too hot)*

136–138   **crowner** coroner (to hold an inquest on – **sit o'** – the 'drowned' Sir Toby)

141   **yond ...** the young man outside

142–144   **he takes on him ...** He says he already knows that, and that's why he has come to see you.

OLIVIA	By mine honour, half drunk. (*To* SIR TOBY) What is he at the gate, cousin?

120

SIR TOBY	A gentleman.

OLIVIA	A gentleman! What gentleman?

SIR TOBY	'T is a gentleman here – a plague o' these pickle-herring! (*To* FESTE) How now, sot!

FESTE	Good Sir Toby!

125

OLIVIA	Cousin, cousin, how have you come so early by this lethargy?

SIR TOBY	Lechery! I defy lechery. There's one at the gate.

OLIVIA	Ay, marry; what is he?

SIR TOBY	Let him be the devil, an he will, I care not; give me faith, say I. Well, it's all one.

130

Exit.

OLIVIA	What's a drunken man like, fool?

FESTE	Like a drowned man, a fool, and a madman; one draught above heat makes him a fool, the second mads him, and a third drowns him.

135

OLIVIA	Go thou and seek the crowner, and let him sit o' my coz; for he's in the third degree of drink, he's drowned; go, look after him.

FESTE	He is but mad yet, madonna; and the fool shall look to the madman.

140

Exit.

Re-enter MALVOLIO.

MALVOLIO	Madam, yond young fellow swears he will speak with you. I told him you were sick; he takes on him to understand so much, and therefore comes to speak with you. I told him you were asleep; he seems to have a foreknowledge of that too, and

145

1.5 Olivia's house

Malvolio describes the persistent young visitor and Olivia agrees to see him.

Activities

Character review: Feste (3)

A From what you have seen of Feste so far:
- What exactly is his 'job'?
- What does his relationship seem to be with Maria; Olivia; Sir Toby?
- What does Malvolio think of him?

B Curio later describes Feste as 'a fool that the lady Olivia's father took much delight in' (2.4.11–12). List the qualities of Feste that you think Olivia's father would have enjoyed, from what you have seen so far. Then write out an advertisement for an expensive magazine headed 'FOOL WANTED FOR LARGE COUNTRY HOUSE ON COAST OF ILLYRIA.'

Start off a list of requirements (Must be able to ...) and add to them as you see more of Feste throughout the play.

C Write two opening paragraphs for a study of Feste, the first on his role in Olivia's household and his relationship with other characters; the second on the nature of his 'foolery' and wit. Look, for example, at Feste's use of proverbial sayings (19), puns (22), paradox (39 ...), mock logic (42–51) and erudition (55–56).

147–148 **He's fortified ...** He won't take no for an answer.

151 **sheriff's post** *Sheriffs' houses had decorated posts outside. Viola is determined to stand there until she is allowed in to see Olivia.*

154 **of mankind** an ordinary person: there's nothing special about him *(more dramatic irony)*

156 **Of very ill manner** extremely rude

158 **Of what personage ...** What does he look like and how old is he?

160 **as a squash is ...** like an unripe pea-pod before it is a pea

161 **codling** an unripe apple

162 **in standing water** at the turning of the tide. *(All Malvolio's phrases suggest that the visitor is no longer a child but is not quite an adult.)*

163 **well-favoured** good-looking

163 **shrewishly** sharply

168 **veil** *Olivia wears a veil as she is still in mourning.*

169 **embassy** official message

172 **Most radiant ...** *Viola has written an overdone speech in praise of Olivia.*

therefore comes to speak with you. What is to be
said to him, lady? He's fortified against any
denial.

OLIVIA   Tell him he shall not speak with me.

MALVOLIO   Has been told so; and he says he'll stand at your   150
            door like a sheriff's post, and be the supporter to
            a bench, but he'll speak with you.

OLIVIA   What kind o' man is he?

MALVOLIO   Why, of mankind.

OLIVIA   What manner of man?   155

MALVOLIO   Of very ill manner; he'll speak with you, will you
            or no.

OLIVIA   Of what personage and years is he?

MALVOLIO   Not yet old enough for a man, nor young enough
            for a boy; as a squash is before 't is a peascod, or a 160
            codling when 't is almost an apple; 't is with him
            in standing water, between boy and man. He is
            very well-favoured, and he speaks very shrewishly;
            one would think his mother's milk were scarce
            out of him.   165

OLIVIA   Let him approach. Call in my gentlewoman.

MALVOLIO   Gentlewoman, my lady calls.

                                                          Exit.

Re-enter MARIA.

OLIVIA   Give me my veil; come, throw it o'er my face.
            We'll once more hear Orsino's embassy.

Enter VIOLA and attendants.

VIOLA   The honourable lady of the house, which is she?   170

OLIVIA   Speak to me; I shall answer for her. Your will?

VIOLA   Most radiant, exquisite, and unmatchable

1.5 Olivia's house

Viola (disguised as Cesario) confidently addresses the two veiled women, first checking which one is Olivia.

Activities

Actors' interpretations (3): gender

Women were not allowed to act on stage in Shakespeare's England, so all the female roles were played by boys or young men.

A Brainstorm all the major qualities that you have noticed in Viola so far. Then, using your knowledge of actors and actresses you have seen on television, stage or films, decide who would be suitable as Viola/Cesario, if you were casting (a) a female, and (b) a male. Give good reasons for your choices and discuss them with other people.

B Hold a class discussion about whether there are such things as 'male qualities' and 'female qualities':

1. Brainstorm all the major qualities and features of behaviour that you have noticed in Viola so far (such as determination or intelligence).

2. Then discuss whether each one seems to be the kind of thing that many people traditionally think of as being a typically 'male' or 'female' quality.

3. How does the presentation of Viola affect your view of the traditional qualities associated with men and with women?

(Continued on page 36)

---

177 **con it** learn it by heart

177 **let me sustain no scorn** don't mock me

178–179 **comptible ...** I'm very sensitive, even to the slightest rudeness.

182 **out of my part** I cannot speak any lines which are not in my part.

182–184 **give me modest assurance** Be reasonable, assure me.

185 **comedian** actor

186–187 **by the very fangs of malice ...** I swear by all that is cruel

187 **I am not that I play** I'm not what I appear to be.

189 **usurp myself** if I haven't wrongfully taken over my position *(of lady of the house)*

191 **what is yours to bestow ...** Your beauty, which is yours to give in marriage, should not be kept to yourself.

192 **from my commission** not part of the message I am supposed to deliver

202–204 **time of moon ...** I am not mad enough myself to join in (**make one in**) such a crazy (**skipping**) conversation.

205–207 **hoist sail ...** *Maria uses an expression from sailing. Viola retorts by calling her a deck-cleaner* (**swabber**) *and declaring that she will moor* (**hull**) *here a while longer.*

beauty – I pray you, tell me if this be the lady of
the house, for I never saw her; I would be loath to
cast away my speech; for besides that it is   175
excellently well penned, I have taken great pains
to con it. Good beauties, let me sustain no scorn;
I am very comptible, even to the least sinister
usage.

OLIVIA   Whence came you, sir?   180

VIOLA   I can say little more than I have studied, and that
              question's out of my part. Good gentle one, give
              me modest assurance if you be the lady of the
              house, that I may proceed in my speech.

OLIVIA   Are you a comedian?   185

VIOLA   No, my profound heart; and yet, by the very fangs
              of malice I swear I am not that I play. Are you the
              lady of the house?

OLIVIA   If I do not usurp myself, I am.

VIOLA   Most certain, if you are she, you *do* usurp yourself;   190
              for what is yours to bestow is not yours to reserve.
              But this is from my commission; I will on with
              my speech in your praise, and then show you the
              heart of my message.

OLIVIA   Come to what is important in 't; I forgive you the   195
              praise.

VIOLA   Alas! I took great pains to study it, and 't is poetical.

OLIVIA   It is the more like to be feigned; I pray you keep it
              in. I heard you were saucy at my gates, and
              allowed your approach, rather to wonder at you   200
              than to hear you. If you be not mad, be gone; if
              you have reason, be brief; 't is not that time of
              moon with me to make one in so skipping a
              dialogue.

MARIA   Will you hoist sail, sir? here lies your way.   205

VIOLA   (*To* MARIA) No, good swabber; I am to hull here a

1.5 Olivia's house

Olivia agrees to listen to Viola–Cesario and sends Maria away.
Viola–Cesario asks to see Olivia's face.

Activities

C Discuss how differently you might react as part of the audience watching an all-male production of the play.

1. Think of what Viola does in Act 1 and discuss which moments you think would be easiest, and which most difficult, for (a) an actress playing Viola, and (b) an actor playing Viola, to act convincingly.

2. How differently might you view the relationships between Viola and Orsino and Cesario and Olivia, if all the actors were male?

207–208 **Some mollification for . . .** Please pacify . . .

209 **. . . your mind** . . . what you want.

211–212 **Sure, you have some hideous matter . . .** You must have something awful to say if you need to be so polite.

212–213 **your office** your business.

214–216 **I bring no overture of war . . .** I am not declaring war nor demanding tribute-money (**homage**); I'm offering peace (**I hold the olive**).

219–220 **The rudeness . . .** I appeared rude because I was treated rudely.

221 **maidenhead** virginity

222 **divinity** holy messages **profanation** blasphemy

224 **text** *extract from the Bible or holy writings on which the sermon will be based.*

226 **A comfortable doctrine** a comforting lesson

227 **Where lies . . . ?** Which book does it come from?

230 **To answer by the method** to use your style of language

231 **heresy** false religious teaching

234–235 **commission . . .** Have you an official order to talk direct to my face?

235–236 **out of your text** You have wandered off your subject.

little longer. (*To* OLIVIA) Some mollification for your giant, sweet lady.

OLIVIA Tell me your mind.

VIOLA I am a messenger.   210

OLIVIA Sure, you have some hideous matter to deliver, when the courtesy of it is so fearful. Speak your office.

VIOLA It alone concerns your ear. I bring no overture of war, no taxation of homage; I hold the olive in   215
my hand; my words are as full of peace as matter.

OLIVIA Yet you began rudely. What are you? What would you?

VIOLA The rudeness that hath appeared in me have I learned from my entertainment. What I am, and   220
what I would, are as secret as maidenhead; to your ears, divinity; to any other's, profanation.

OLIVIA Give us the place alone; we will hear this divinity.

Exeunt MARIA and attendants.

Now, sir; what is your text?

VIOLA Most sweet lady –   225

OLIVIA A comfortable doctrine, and much may be said of it. Where lies your text?

VIOLA In Orsino's bosom.

OLIVIA In his bosom! In what chapter of his bosom?

VIOLA To answer by the method, in the first of his heart. 230

OLIVIA O! I have read it; it is heresy. Have you no more to say?

VIOLA Good madam, let me see your face.

OLIVIA Have you any commission from your lord to negotiate with my face? You are now out of your   235

1.5 Olivia's house

Viola–Cesario admires Olivia's beauty, but Olivia says that she cannot return Orsino's love.

Activities

Character review: Orsino (2)

Olivia lists a number of Orsino's qualities in lines 261–265.

Draw up three columns. List the virtues as Olivia names them in the first column; write the modern explanations of those virtues in the second column; and in the third, either find evidence in the play to support what she has said about him, or think of a way in which such a quality might be displayed in his daily life.

237 **such a one I was ...** 'This is what I looked like at this date' (**this present**).

239 **if God did all** if it's natural

240 **in grain** it's indelible (it won't wash off)

241 **truly blent** perfectly blended

242 **cunning** clever, skilful

247 **divers schedules** various sale catalogues

248 **inventoried** listed **particle and utensil** household object

249 *Item* This word used to appear in front of each item on a list.

249–250 **indifferent red** reddish

255–257 **O! such love ...** O, you might return such love, even if you were crowned as the most beautiful woman in the world.

257 **nonpareil** unequalled

258 **fertile tears** gushing tears

261 **I suppose him** I believe him to be

262–265 **Of great estate** of very high rank, virtuous (**of fresh and stainless youth**), well spoken of (**In voices well divulged**), generous (**free**), learned and courageous; and an attractive and physically graceful person.

267 **in my master's flame** as passionately as my master does

268 **such a deadly life** *Orsino is experiencing 'a living death'.*

text; but we will draw the curtain and show you
the picture. Look you, sir; such a one I was this
present; is 't not well done? (*Unveiling*)

VIOLA   Excellently done, if God did all.

OLIVIA   'T is in grain, sir; 't will endure wind and weather.   240

VIOLA   'T is beauty truly blent, whose red and white
Nature's own sweet and cunning hand laid on;
Lady, you are the cruell'st she alive,
If you will lead these graces to the grave
And leave the world no copy.   245

OLIVIA   O, sir, I will not be so hard-hearted! I will give out
divers schedules of my beauty; it shall be
inventoried, and every particle and utensil
labelled to my will, as, *Item*, Two lips indifferent
red; *Item*, Two grey eyes with lids to them; *Item*,   250
One neck, one chin, and so forth. Were you sent
hither to praise me?

VIOLA   I see you what you are; you are too proud;
But, if you were the devil, you are fair.
My lord and master loves you; O! such love   255
Could be but recompensed, though you were
    crowned
The nonpareil of beauty.

OLIVIA   How does he love me?

VIOLA   With adorations, fertile tears,
With groans that thunder love, with sighs of fire.

OLIVIA   Your lord does know my mind; I cannot love him;   260
Yet I suppose him virtuous, know him noble,
Of great estate, of fresh and stainless youth;
In voices well divulged, free, learned, and valiant;
And in dimension and the shape of nature
A gracious person; but yet I cannot love him;   265
He might have took his answer long ago.

VIOLA   If I did love you in my master's flame,
With such a suffering, such a deadly life,
In your denial I would find no sense;

ivia's house

*Having explained what she would do if she loved Olivia herself,
Viola–Cesario leaves, and Olivia realises that she is falling in love.*

Activities

Character review: Viola (1)

'Make me a willow cabin ...' In
Viola/Cesario's famous speech
(271–279), she sets out what she would
do if she were wooing Olivia. Thinking
perhaps of what she would be prepared
to do in pursuit of her love for Orsino,
she lists a number of easily visualised
activities. First re-read and then perform
Viola's speech – learn it if you can.

A List in your own words the extremes to
which, in Viola's eyes, a real lover will
go in trying to win a person's love.

B Create a collage, using images cut from
magazines, or your own artwork, to
illustrate the lines, or to reflect their
mood. Try to echo the theme of love
which runs through the play.

C Discuss what this speech reveals about
Viola and the nature of love, as she
experiences it. What happens when we
set this declaration against Orsino's
passion?

271 **willow** *symbol of unrequited
(unreturned) love*

272 **my soul** *Orsino's soul has
been given to Olivia, and is in
the house with her.*

273 **loyal cantons** faithful songs
of rejected (**contemnéd**) love

275 **Holla your name ...** shout
out your name to the echoing
(**reverberate**) hills

281 **Above my fortunes ...** I
come from a good family (**my
state is well**), even though at
present things are not going
well for me.

287 **fee'd post** paid messenger

288 **My master ...** It's my master
you should be rewarding ...

289–291 **Love make his heart ...** I
hope love turns his heart to
flint and that you love him;
and that your passion
(**fervour**) is treated with
contempt, as his is now!

295 **Thy tongue** your speech

296 **blazon** coat of arms

296 **soft!** wait a minute! slow
down!

297 **Unless the master ...** I wish
Cesario were in Orsino's place
(in love with me).
*Cesario's attractive qualities
(**perfections**) are like an
illness that can be caught,
without realising it (**With an
invisible and subtle stealth**),
through the eyes.*

	I would not understand it.	
OLIVIA	Why, what would you?	270

VIOLA Make me a willow cabin at your gate,
And call upon my soul within the house;
Write loyal cantons of contemnéd love,
And sing them loud even in the dead of night;
Holla your name to the reverberate hills, 275
And make the babbling gossip of the air
Cry out "Olivia!" O, you should not rest
Between the elements of air and earth,
But you should pity me.

OLIVIA You might do much. What is your parentage? 280

VIOLA Above my fortunes, yet my state is well;
I am a gentleman.

OLIVIA Get you to your lord;
I cannot love him. Let him send no more,
Unless, perchance, *you* come to me again,
To tell me how he takes it. Fare you well; 285
I thank you for your pains; (*She gives* VIOLA *a bag of
money*) spend this for me.

VIOLA I am no fee'd post, lady; keep your purse;
My master, not myself, lacks recompense.
Love make his heart of flint that you shall love,
And let your fervour, like my master's, be 290
Placed in contempt! Farewell, fair cruelty.

Exit.

OLIVIA "What is your parentage?"
"Above my fortunes, yet my state is well;
I am a gentleman." I'll be sworn thou art;
Thy tongue, thy face, thy limbs, actions, and spirit, 295
Do give thee five-fold blazon. Not too fast; soft!
soft! –
Unless the master were the man ... How now!
Even so quickly may one catch the plague?
Methinks I feel this youth's perfections,
With an invisible and subtle stealth 300

41

)livia's house

Olivia sends Malvolio after 'Orsino's man' to return a ring and sends a message that she is willing to see him again.

Activities

Character review: Olivia (3)

A Discuss your early impressions of Olivia. Recap first on:
- what Orsino says about her in scene 1
- what the Sea Captain says in scene 2.

Then discuss what we learn, when she appears, about:
- her attitude to Feste and the effect that Feste has upon her
- her attitude to Malvolio
- her reaction to Cesario when 'he' first appears
- her feelings at the end of the scene.

B From the point of Viola's arrival, Olivia's feelings undergo some dramatic changes.

Go through the script, jotting down what you think Olivia is thinking or feeling at different points in the conversation, up to Viola's exit (lines 170–291). (There is an example of how to annotate a script on page 222.)

C Maria later (2.3.128–130) tells Sir Toby: 'since the youth of the count's was today with my lady, she is much out of quiet' (unsettled).

Discuss what changes in her behaviour Maria might have observed. (What was she like before Cesario's arrival?)

303 **peevish** stubborn, awkward

304 **The County's man** the Count's servant

305 **Would I or not ...** Whether I wanted it or not. Tell him I won't accept it (**I'll none of it**).

306–307 **Desire him not to flatter ...** Ask him not to give his lord any encouraging or hopeful words: I am not going to be his wife.

309 **I'll give him reasons ...** I will explain my actions. *(Olivia is deliberately speaking in riddles, so that Cesario will understand her meaning, but Malvolio will not.)*

309 **Hie thee** Hurry!

311–312 **I do I know not what ...** I don't know what I'm doing, and I am worried that my reason (**mind**) might have been misled by my eye (into falling in love at first sight).

313–314 **Fate ...** *Olivia asks Fate to take control.*

313–314 **ourselves we do not owe** We do not 'own ourselves' (have power over our own destinies). Whatever is destined to happen (**decreed**) will happen – so let this happen.

To creep in at mine eyes. Well, let it be.
What, ho! Malvolio!

Re-enter MALVOLIO.

MALVOLIO   Here, madam, at your service.

OLIVIA   Run after that same peevish messenger,
The County's man; he left this ring behind him,
Would I or not; tell him I'll none of it.   305
Desire him not to flatter with his lord,
Nor hold him up with hopes; I am not for him.
If that the youth will come this way tomorrow,
I'll give him reasons for 't. Hie thee, Malvolio.

MALVOLIO   Madam, I will.   310

Exit.

OLIVIA   I do I know not what, and fear to find
Mine eye too great a flatterer for my mind.
Fate, show thy force; ourselves we do not owe;
What is decreed must be, and be this so.

Exit.

Exam practice

Character review: Orsino (3)

(A) Look back at scene 1. Then jot down (a) everything you know about Orsino; and (b) what your impressions and feelings are about him, at first sight.

(B) The Captain makes the point that ordinary people always gossip about the nobility. Write a short article about Orsino for a magazine such as *Hello!*, telling people about Orsino's lifestyle, his attitudes to love, and his interest in Olivia. Imagine that you have interviewed people like Valentine and Curio, as well as some of Olivia's servants, and include some of their comments in your article. Find some suitable photographs of people to represent your picture of Orsino and Olivia.

(C) Make notes for a piece of writing to be completed later on Orsino. What do the following reveal about Orsino the man and his feelings for Olivia, in your opinion:

- his use of imperatives, exclamations and rhetorical questions
- the nature of the imagery he uses in describing love generally, and his love for Olivia in particular
- the comments he makes about Olivia's feelings
- his exit couplet?

Actors' interpretations (4): gender

Because we know that Cesario is actually a woman (while the characters treat her as a young man), we are encouraged to think about the differences between men and women: the biological differences, their different lives in Shakespeare's time (and our own), and the different attitudes that people have towards them. Remember also that there were no women actors in Shakespeare's time: all female roles were played by boys or young men.

(A) Hot-seat Valentine, asking him questions about Cesario. Assume that Valentine was present when Orsino first interviewed Cesario. Ask what he knows about Cesario's past, what Cesario said at the interview which helped him to get such a good post in Orsino's service, and what the other courtiers think of his growing relationship with Orsino. What jobs is 'he' expected to do?

(B) Often in Shakespeare's plays, the audience will know something that the characters don't know. When this happens, we call it dramatic irony. At several points in *Twelfth Night*, characters say something on the assumption that Cesario is a man, while we know that 'he' is a woman. Orsino's comments on Cesario's feminine good looks are a good example. Imagine you are directing *Twelfth Night*. Annotate

Act 1, scene 4 to help the actors perform this scene effectively (paying particular attention to lines 29–36).

You could give advice on:

- movements and actions
- how to speak the lines (e.g. shouting, whispering, etc.)
- where to pause
- facial expressions
- how the characters are feeling

c Make notes on the features of the play so far which have raised questions concerning gender. Discuss the following, for example:

- How are the lives of the male and female characters different?
- What do Viola and Olivia have in common?
- What do Orsino and Aguecheek have in common?
- What kinds of conflict exist between the men and the women?

Think particularly about cross-dressing:

- What plot opportunities are offered when the central female character disguises herself as a man? What can she now do, that she could not do before? What potential for comedy now exists? Which points about gender can now be made?

How different do you think it might be to see an all-male production, where a young man plays a woman who disguises herself as a young man? (This is, of course, how audiences would have seen the play performed in Shakespeare's time, when there were no women actors.)

Character review: relationships

1. Discuss as a class what the following pairs of characters seem to think of each other, supporting your ideas with evidence from the script, and keeping notes:
   - Sir Toby and Sir Andrew
   - Maria and Sir Andrew
   - Malvolio and Feste
   - Olivia and Feste
   - Olivia and Malvolio.

2. Discuss in groups what the social status of the various characters seems to be.
   1. What are the differences in rank between Olivia and Orsino? How significant are they (see 1.3.104–106, for example)?
   2. What does Malvolio's function seem to be in Olivia's household? How important is he? What powers does he have?
   3. What is Maria's status? How is she labelled by Sir Toby (1.3.50) and how does this square with her behaviour when Cesario arrives?
   4. What is Feste's role in Olivia's household? In particular, what can he get away with, and what is likely to get him into trouble?

2.1 The sea-coast

Antonio, a sea captain, has rescued Viola's brother Sebastian from the shipwreck, and offers to be his servant. Sebastian tells him about Viola.

Activities

Character review: relationships
Antonio and Sebastian? (1)

A Discuss what we know about these two new characters. From what they say to each other, what do you suppose has happened to them since the shipwreck?

B Look carefully at the dialogue between Sebastian and Antonio and discuss exactly what kind of friendship is being portrayed here. Sebastian presumably feels gratitude, but what else? Antonio is sympathetic to the young man's plight, but does it go more deeply than that?

1–2 **nor will you not ...** and don't you want me to come with you?

3–5 **My stars shine darkly ...** My birth-stars are bringing me bad luck; my evil fortune (**the malignancy of my fate**) might infect (**distemper**) yours.

6–8 **It were a bad recompense ...** It would be a poor way of repaying you for your love, to burden you with my bad luck.

9 **whither you are bound** where you are going

10–11 **No, sooth ...** Certainly not. My travel plan (**my determinate voyage**) is simply to wander around (**mere extravagancy**).

11–13 **But I perceive in you ...** But I can see that you are so polite that you will not force (**extort**) from me what I want to hide.

13–15 **it charges me in manners ...** I ought to be good-mannered too.

16 *It is not clear why Sebastian had been calling himself Roderigo.*

19–21 **if the heavens ...** I wish to heaven we had both died together too!

21 **some hour** an hour or so

22 **breach** surf

28–29 **thus far I will boldly ...** I will go as far as to say this ...

29–30 **she bore a mind ...** Even envious people admitted that she was a wonderful person.

32 **drown her remembrance ...** *He 'drowns' her memory with his tears.*

Act 2

Scene 1

The sea-coast.

Enter ANTONIO and SEBASTIAN.

ANTONIO   Will you stay no longer, nor will you not that I go
with you?

SEBASTIAN By your patience, no. My stars shine darkly over
me; the malignancy of my fate might, perhaps,
distemper yours; therefore I shall crave of you   5
your leave that I may bear my evils alone. It were
a bad recompense for your love, to lay any of
them on you.

ANTONIO   Let me yet know of you whither you are bound.

SEBASTIAN No, sooth, sir; my determinate voyage is mere   10
extravagancy. But I perceive in you so excellent a
touch of modesty, that you will not extort from
me what I am willing to keep in; therefore it
charges me in manners the rather to express
myself. You must know of me then, Antonio, my   15
name is Sebastian, which I called Roderigo. My
father was that Sebastian of Messaline, whom I
know you have heard of. He left behind him
myself and a sister, both born in an hour; if the
heavens had been pleased, would we had so   20
ended! but you, sir, altered that; for some hour
before you took me from the breach of the sea
was my sister drowned.

ANTONIO   Alas the day!

SEBASTIAN A lady, sir, though it was said she much   25
resembled me, was yet of many accounted
beautiful; but, though I could not with such
estimable wonder overfar believe that, yet thus far
I will boldly publish her: she bore a mind that
Envy could not but call fair. She is drowned   30
already, sir, with salt water, though I seem to
drown her remembrance again with more.

ANTONIO   Pardon me, sir, your bad entertainment.

Near Olivia's house

Although Antonio has enemies in Olivia's court, he decides to follow Sebastian. In Scene 2 Malvolio catches up with Viola–Cesario and tries to 'return' the ring.

Activities

Actors' interpretations (5): Viola

Actors don't only have their characters to think about: sometimes they have decisions to make about props too. Zoe Wanamaker had problems with the ring: 'On her way back from Olivia's house, she is overtaken by Malvolio with the ring ... What to do with this ring was the source of some discussion during our rehearsals, for it is never given back or referred to again. Eventually it was decided that I should hang it on a twig of the stage tree where it is found again by Feste at the end of the play.'

Discuss what else could be done with it.

Character review: Viola (2)

Viola's long soliloquy at the end of 2.2 is an important turning point. Annotate the speech, to show the different thoughts, ideas and realisations which come to mind, line by line. For example:

puzzled about the conversation with M.	I left no ring with her ...
begins to realise ...	Fortune forbid ...

38 **recovered** saved

39–40 **my bosom is full ...** I feel very emotional.

40–42 **I am yet so near ...** I am so close to womanly behaviour **(the manners of my mother)** that it will not take much for me to start crying.

44 **gentleness** favour, support

47 **But, come what may** I don't care what happens to me.

1 **even now** just now

2–3 **on a moderate pace ...** Walking reasonably fast, I have only got this far.

6–7 **put your lord into ...** Make your lord certain that there is no hope that she will marry him.

9 **hardy** bold

11 **I'll none of it** I don't want it.

SEBASTIAN O good Antonio! forgive me your trouble.

ANTONIO If you will not murder me for my love, let me be   35
your servant.

SEBASTIAN If you will not undo what you have done, that is,
kill him whom you have recovered, desire it not.
Fare ye well at once; my bosom is full of
kindness; and I am yet so near the manners of my   40
mother that upon the least occasion more mine
eyes will tell tales of me. I am bound to the Count
Orsino's court; farewell.

Exit.

ANTONIO The gentleness of all the gods go with thee.
I have many enemies in Orsino's court,   45
Else would I very shortly see thee there;
But, come what may, I do adore thee so,
That danger shall seem sport, and I will go.

Exit.

Scene 2

A street.

Enter VIOLA; MALVOLIO following.

MALVOLIO Were you not even now with the Countess Olivia?

VIOLA Even now, sir; on a moderate pace I have since
arrived but hither.

MALVOLIO She returns this ring to you, sir; you might have
saved me my pains, to have taken it away   5
yourself. She adds, moreover, that you should put
your lord into a desperate assurance she will none
of him. And one thing more: that you be never so
hardy to come again in his affairs, unless it be to
report your lord's taking of this. Receive it so.   10

He throws the ring on the ground.

VIOLA She took the ring of me; I'll none of it.

2.3 Olivia's house: late at night

Viola realises that Olivia must have fallen in love with her. When Scene 3 opens Sir Toby and Sir Andrew are up late, drinking.

Activities

Themes (3): time

A 1. How many recent songs can you think of which refer to time in their titles or lyrics?

2. List the five main things which the quotations or song lyrics say about time (for example, that time always passes, no matter what we do).

3. Try to fit some of these quotations into the situations that characters find themselves in here. (Which quotation would best fit Olivia, for example?)

B When Viola says: 'O time, thou must untangle this, not I; It is too hard a knot for me to untie' she seems to think that time has the ability to sort things out.

Does time untangle things in real life? Predict the ways in which 'time' will affect the characters in the play:

• What kinds of complications can ensue?

• Who will be happier with the passing of time – because it will sort out difficulties – and who will be less happy?

C Theme database: Start collecting references on the theme of time. For each one, note what power time is claimed to possess and why the character refers to time at that particular moment.

12 **peevishly** rudely

17 **Fortune forbid my outside hath not . . .** I hope she has not been attracted by my appearance!

19–20 **methought her eyes had lost her tongue . . .** because she was staring at me, she couldn't speak properly

21–22 **the cunning of her passion . . .** She has used this rude messenger as a clever way of giving me an invitation.

27 **the pregnant enemy** the devil, full (**pregnant**) of cunning ideas

28–29 **How easy is it . . .** Isn't it easy for handsome but deceitful men (**the proper-false**) to make an impression on women's hearts.

30–31 **our frailty . . .** Our weakness is the problem: that's the way we are made.

32 **How will this fadge?** How will this turn out?

33 **fond** *a much stronger word in Shakespeare's time*

35–36 **As I am man . . .** While I am pretending to be a man, it is hopeless to try to win my master's love.

38 **thriftless** useless, profitless

2 **betimes** early

2 ***diluculo surgere*** *part of a Latin proverb meaning that getting up early is good for you*

MALVOLIO   Come, sir, you peevishly threw it to her; and her
will is it should be so returned; if it be worth
stooping for, there it lies in your eye; if not, be it
his that finds it.   15

Exit.

VIOLA   I left no ring with her; what means this lady?
Fortune forbid my outside have not charmed her!
She made good view of me; indeed so much
That sure methought her eyes had lost her tongue,
For she did speak in starts distractedly.   20
She loves me, sure; the cunning of her passion
Invites me in this churlish messenger.
None of my lord's ring! Why, he sent her none.
Ha   I am the <u>man</u>; if it be so, as 't is,
Poor lady, she were better love a dream.   25
Disguise, I see thou art a wickedness
Wherein the pregnant enemy does much.
How easy is it for the proper-false
In women's waxen hearts to set their forms!
Alas! our frailty is the cause, not we,   30
For such as we are made of, such we be.
How will this fadge? My master loves her dearly;
And I, poor monster, fond as much on him;   ← Plot
And she, mistaken, seems to dote on me.
What will become of this? As I am man,   35
My state is desperate for my master's love;
As I am woman – now alas the day! –
What thriftless sighs shall poor Olivia breathe!
O time, thou must untangle this, not I;
It is too hard a knot for me to untie.   40

Exit.

Scene 3

A room in Olivia's house.

Enter SIR TOBY BELCH and SIR ANDREW AGUECHEEK.

SIR TOBY   Approach, Sir Andrew: not to be a-bed after
midnight is to be up betimes; and *diluculo surgere*,
thou knowest –

2.3 Olivia's house: late at night

Feste joins Sir Toby and Sir Andrew and they admire his previous night's jesting.

Activities

Themes (4): time

A major message of 'O mistress mine' is something like: 'Enjoy life while you're still young!' You might sometimes hear this described as the *carpe diem* theme (*carpe diem* literally means 'seize' – or 'grab hold of' – 'the day'). Re-read the lyrics and compare them with the messages of today's popular songs. Do any modern songs echo the *carpe diem* theme?

Character review: Feste (4)

Stephen Boxer, who played Feste in 1997, said: 'Youth's a stuff will not endure – grab it while you can. I don't think this is a young fool.' Is Feste old, in your opinion? (Shakespeare doesn't tell us, but there is possibly a clue in 1.5.113–114.)

Discuss how old you think Feste and the other major characters are.

---

6 **A false conclusion ...** Bad reasoning: I hate it like an empty beer-mug. *Toby's logic is that, if you stay up late enough, it becomes early.*

9–10 **... the four elements** *Elizabethans believed that everything was made up of the four elements of earth, water, fire and air.*

14 **Marian** *Another name for Maria. She is also called Mary.*

14 **stoup** large jug

16–17 **the picture of 'we three'** *This used to be a popular inn sign, showing two fools, or asses (with the viewer making the third fool).*

18 **a catch** *a song sung as a round*

19 **breast** singing voice

22 **in very gracious fooling** You were cracking some good jokes.

23–25 **Pigrogromitus ...** *All these names were presumably invented by Feste to impress Sir Andrew.*

26 **leman** sweetheart

27–29 **impeticos ...** *Feste's ridiculous way of saying 'I put your tip (**gratillity**) in the pocket of my long-coat.' The rest of his speech is almost pure nonsense.*

34 **testril** sixpence

SIR ANDREW	Nay, by my troth, I know not; but I know, to be up late is to be up late.

5

SIR TOBY	A false conclusion; I hate it as an unfilled can. To be up after midnight, and to go to bed then, is early; so that to go to bed after midnight is to go to bed betimes. Does not our life consist of the four elements?

10

SIR ANDREW Faith, so they say; but I think it rather consists of eating and drinking.

SIR TOBY Thou 'rt a scholar; let us therefore eat and drink. (*Calling*) Marian, I say! a stoup of wine!

Enter FESTE.

SIR ANDREW Here comes the fool, i' faith.

15

FESTE How now, my hearts! Did you never see the picture of "we three"?

SIR TOBY Welcome, ass. Now let's have a catch.

SIR ANDREW By my troth, the fool has an excellent breast. I had rather than forty shillings I had such a leg, and so sweet a breath to sing, as the fool has. (*To FESTE*) In sooth, thou wast in very gracious fooling last night, when thou spokest of Pigrogromitus, of the Vapians passing the equinoctial of Queubus; 't was very good, i' faith. I sent thee sixpence for thy leman; hadst it?

20

25

FESTE I did impeticos thy gratillity, for Malvolio's nose is no whip-stock; my lady has a white hand, and the Myrmidons are no bottle-ale houses.

SIR ANDREW Excellent! Why, this is the best fooling, when all is done. Now, a song.

30

SIR TOBY Come on; there is sixpence for you; let's have a song.

SIR ANDREW There's a testril of me too; if one knight give a –

2.3 Olivia's house: late at night

Feste sings a song with the message that love should be enjoyed now, not in some uncertain future time.

Activities

Actors' interpretations (6): Malvolio's entrance

In the 1969 RSC production, Toby and Maria were dancing at this point (line 82), Feste playing his guitar and Sir Andrew the bagpipes. Donald Sinden, who played Malvolio, describes his entrance:

'At my very fastest walk, I eject myself from the right. Arriving in the centre of the group, Feste on my left, Aguecheek down-centre,* Sir Toby up-centre, and Maria standing on a chair, right, the "music" continues until one by one they become aware of my presence ... first Feste, then Maria who signals to Toby who sits centre, then Aguecheek who subsides onto the floor ... Passing my glower from Aguecheek back to Feste, I suddenly become aware that my coat has flown open exposing my "shorty" nightgown and my bare legs beneath it! With a lightning movement, I cross the coat over my shame and at the same moment one knee slightly crosses the other.'

(* 'down' is near the front of the stage; 'up' near the back)

(Continued on page 56)

35–38 **A song of good life** *is a drinking song; Sir Andrew thinks he means a song about virtue.*

42 **trip** skip

47–52 **'T is not hereafter ...** not in some uncertain future time

49 **still** always

50 **In delay ...** There's no point in putting it off.

52 **Youth's a stuff ...** You don't stay young for ever.

53 **mellifluous** as sweet as honey

54 **contagious breath** catchy tune

56 **To hear by the nose ...** If we could hear through our noses, the tune would be sweet (**dulcet**) in the way it infects us.

57 **welkin** skies

58–59 **weaver** *Weavers were known for being religious people who sang psalms as they worked. The three souls are from the three singers.*

60 **An** if

60 **I am a dog at** I'm good at

61 **some dogs will catch well** *Feste's wordplay: (1) hounds are good at catching; (2) they will sing a 'catch'.*

62–67 *The full title of the song is 'Hold thy peace, thou knave' ('Shut up, you villain'). Feste jokes that, if he sings it, he will be forced (**constrained**) to call Sir Andrew a knave; and he can never start singing if he 'holds his peace'.*

Act 2 Scene 3

FESTE	Would you have a love-song, or a song of good life?	35
SIR TOBY	A love-song, a love-song.	
SIR ANDREW	Ay, ay; I care not for good life.	

FESTE (*Sings*)

> *O mistress mine! where are you roaming?*
> *O stay and hear! your true love's coming,*   40
>   *That can sing both high and low.*
> *Trip no further, pretty sweeting;*
> *Journeys end in lovers meeting,*
>   *Every wise man's son doth know.*

SIR ANDREW	Excellent good, i' faith.	45
SIR TOBY	Good, good.	

FESTE (*Sings*)

> *What is love? 'T is not hereafter;*
> *Present mirth hath present laughter;*
>   *What's to come is still unsure.*
> *In delay there lies no plenty;*   50
> *Then come kiss me, sweet-and-twenty,*
>   *Youth's a stuff will not endure.*

SIR ANDREW	A mellifluous voice, as I am true knight.	
SIR TOBY	A contagious breath.	
SIR ANDREW	Very sweet and contagious, i' faith.	55
SIR TOBY	To hear by the nose, it is dulcet in contagion. But shall we make the welkin dance indeed? Shall we rouse the night-owl in a catch that will draw three souls out of one weaver? Shall we do that?	
SIR ANDREW	An you love me, let's do 't; I am dog at a catch.	60
FESTE	By 'r lady, sir, and some dogs will catch well.	
SIR ANDREW	Most certain. Let our catch be, "Thou knave".	
FESTE	"Hold thy peace, thou knave", knight? I shall be constrained in 't to call thee knave, knight.	

(handwritten note: nobody smells good.)

2.3 Olivia's house: late at night

Feste, Sir Toby and Sir Andrew sing together and Malvolio, disturbed by this noise, comes down to rebuke them.

Activities

What are your opinions of Malvolio from earlier appearances? Do you find him objectionable, for example? Or can you have some sympathy for him in his position in Olivia's household?

A Draw a sketch of Malvolio as you think he ought to look when he enters. Decide first whether he should look comic or threatening (or both?), and whether he has just got out of bed.

B Act out the scene as Donald Sinden describes it, or freeze-frame the moment of Malvolio's entrance. Then discuss other ways in which it might be done and try out one of them.

C 1. Discuss what happened in this 1969 production (a) to show that Toby and the others are afraid of Malvolio; (b) to make Malvolio a figure of fun.
2. What do (a) and (b) suggest about the overall approach to the Malvolio plot in the 1969 production?
3. How would you create quite a different effect (for example, to create some sympathy for Malvolio at this point)?

69 **caterwauling** terrible noise

72–73 **My lady's a Cataian ...** *Sir Toby is drunk and answers with defiant nonsense, using phrases taken from popular songs.* **We are politicians** *might mean that they are clever enough to deal with Malvolio.*

74 **consanguineous** a blood-relative *(of Olivia)*

75 **Tillyvally** *A nonsense word, showing his contempt.*

77 **Beshrew me ...** Damn me, but Sir Toby's on good form with his jokes!

78 **... disposed** in the right mood

79 **with a better grace** He's better at being a fool, but I do it more naturally.

84 **wit** common sense

84 **honesty** sense of 'proper' behaviour

87 **coziers' catches** cobblers' songs

87–88 **without any mitigation ...** without showing consideration by lowering your voices

90 **Sneck up!** Go and hang yourself!

91 **I must be round** I must speak plainly to you.

92–93 Though she looks after (**harbours**) you because you are a relative, she wants nothing to do with your disorderly behaviour.

Sir andrew	'T is not the first time I have constrained one to call 65 me knave. Begin, fool; it begins "Hold thy peace".
Feste	I shall never begin if I hold my peace.
Sir andrew	Good, i' faith. Come, begin.

They sing a catch.

Enter MARIA.

Maria	What a caterwauling do you keep here! If my lady have not called up her steward Malvolio and bid 70 him turn you out of doors, never trust me.
Sir toby	My lady's a Cataian; we are politicians; Malvolio's a Peg-a-Ramsey, and "Three merry men be we". Am not I consanguineous? Am I not of her blood? Tillyvally; lady! (*Singing*) *There dwelt a* 75 *man in Babylon, lady, lady!* –
Feste	Beshrew me, the knight's in admirable fooling.
Sir andrew	Ay, he does well enough if he be disposed, and so do I too. He does it with a better grace, but I do it more natural. 80
Sir toby (*Singing*)	*O! the twelfth day of December* –
Maria	For the love o' God, peace!

Enter MALVOLIO.

Malvolio	My masters, are you mad, or what are you? Have you no wit, manners, nor honesty, but to gabble like tinkers at this time of night? Do ye make an 85 alehouse of my lady's house, that ye squeak out your coziers' catches without any mitigation or remorse of voice? Is there no respect of place, persons, nor time in you?
Sir toby	We did keep time, sir, in our catches. Sneck up! 90
Malvolio	Sir Toby, I must be round with you. My lady bade me tell you that, though she harbours you as her

2.3 Olivia's house: late at night

Malvolio tells Sir Toby that Olivia wants him to improve his behaviour or leave the house. Sir Toby angrily challenges Malvolio for his puritanical attitude.

Activities

Character review: Malvolio (1)

A Discuss the impression you have formed of Malvolio from his behaviour with Feste in 1.5.75–98 and from what he does and says in this scene.

Desmond Barrit as Malvolio in 1997

95 **misdemeanours** bad behaviour

101 **Is 't even so?** So that's the way you want to behave!

104 **much credit** *(sarcastically)* This is really showing you in a good light.

109–112 **Art any more ...** *Sir Toby is attacking Malvolio for two things: (1) the fact that he is only a steward, but presumes to order them around; (2) his Puritan belief that enjoying yourself* (**cakes and ale**) *is somehow wrong.*

113 **ginger** *made the ale spicy*

116 **rub your chain ...** Go and polish your chain! *Sir Toby again reminds Malvolio that he is no more than a steward (who would wear a chain of office).*

118–121 **if you prized ...** *Malvolio threatens Maria that he will report her to Olivia for supplying the drink which allows this disorderly behaviour to happen* (**means for this uncivil rule**).

(Continued on page 60)

kinsman, she's nothing allied to your disorders. If
you can separate yourself and your
misdemeanours, you are welcome to the house; if   95
not, an it would please you to take leave of her,
she is very willing to bid you farewell.

SIR TOBY (*Singing*)
   Farewell, dear heart, since I must needs be gone.

MARIA   Nay, good Sir Toby.

FESTE (*Singing*)
   His eyes do show his days are almost done.   100

MALVOLIO   Is 't even so?

SIR TOBY (*Singing*)
   But I will never die.

FESTE   Sir Toby, there you lie.

MALVOLIO   This is much credit to you.

SIR TOBY (*Singing in turn*)
   Shall I bid him go?   105

FESTE   *What an if you do?*

SIR TOBY   *Shall I bid him go, and spare not?*

FESTE   *O! no, no, no, no, you dare not.*

SIR TOBY   (*To* FESTE) Out o' tune, sir! ye lie. (*To* MALVOLIO) Art
              any more than a steward? Dost thou think,   110
              because thou art virtuous, there shall be no more
              cakes and ale?

FESTE   Yes, by Saint Anne; and ginger shall be hot i' the
              mouth too.

SIR TOBY   (*To* FESTE) Thou 'rt i' the right. (*To* MALVOLIO) Go,   115
              sir, rub your chain with crumbs. A stoup of wine,
              Maria!

MALVOLIO   Mistress Mary, if you prized my lady's favour at
              any thing more than contempt, you would not

2.3 Olivia's house: late at night

Malvolio leaves, threatening to report Maria to Olivia. Maria declares that Malvolio is not a true puritan but is certainly conceited.

Activities

B As part of his preparation to play a character, the actor Philip Voss writes down everything that he can find in the play, including things that the character says about himself and things that other characters say about him.

Make a list, using your own words, of the facts that he might have learned, when he was preparing to play Malvolio, from Maria's description in 2.3.142–149.

C When Donald Sinden prepared to play Malvolio, he planned down to the last detail where the laughs would come and how big they would be; Desmond Barritt's Malvolio was also very funny – almost a pantomime figure. Philip Voss, on the other hand, never plays for laughs, and his Malvolio was more serious.

1. Discuss (a) how these differences in interpretation would be apparent in some of his appearances in Acts 1, 2 and 3; and (b) how the actor might show the differences.

2. Act out some of these different interpretations and consider which seem to you to be most consistent with your interpretation of the character and the play as a whole. Much will depend on whether Malvolio is played as a more or less comic figure.

123–125 **'T were as good a deed ...** *Sir Andrew's pathetic idea of a joke is to challenge Malvolio to a duel and then not turn up.*

130 **out of quiet** unsettled

131–132 **gull him into a nayword** play such a trick on him that people will come to use his name to mean 'fool'

132 **common recreation** a source of entertainment for the public

135 **Possess us** Tell us what you know.

136 **puritan** *a religious extremist who disapproved of people enjoying themselves (see page 211)*

138 **exquisite** perfect, precise

142–148 **The devil a puritan ...** I'll be damned if he's a real Puritan, or anything consistently (**constantly**), but changes according to what will help him to get on (**a time-pleaser**); he is a pompous (**affectioned**) ass who learns posh language by heart (**cons state**) and repeats it in great chunks (**swarths**); he is extremely conceited (**best persuaded of himself**), and so full – as he thinks – of perfections (**excellences**) that his central belief (**grounds of faith**) is that everybody who sees him loves him.

149 **notable cause** a very good reason

give means for this uncivil rule; she shall know of   120
it, by this hand.

Exit.

MARIA	Go shake your ears.

SIR ANDREW 'T were as good a deed as to drink when a man's
a-hungry, to challenge him the field, and then to
break promise with him and make a fool of him.   125

SIR TOBY Do 't, knight; I'll write thee a challenge; or I'll
deliver thy indignation to him by word of mouth.

MARIA Sweet Sir Toby, be patient for tonight; since the
youth of the count's was today with my lady, she
is much out of quiet. For Monsieur Malvolio, let   130
me alone with him; if I do not gull him into a
nayword, and make him a common recreation,
do not think I have wit enough to lie straight in
my bed. I know I can do it.

SIR TOBY Possess us, possess us. Tell us something of him.   135

MARIA Marry, sir, sometimes he is a kind of puritan.

SIR ANDREW O! if I thought that, I'd beat him like a dog.

SIR TOBY What, for being a puritan? Thy exquisite reason,
dear knight!

SIR ANDREW I have no exquisite reason for 't, but I have reason   140
good enough.

MARIA The devil a puritan that he is, or anything
constantly, but a time-pleaser; an affectioned ass,
that cons state without book, and utters it by
great swarths; the best persuaded of himself; so   145
crammed, as he thinks, with excellences, that it is
his grounds of faith that all that look on him love
him; and on that vice in him will my revenge find
notable cause to work.

SIR TOBY What wilt thou do?   150

2.3 Olivia's house: late at night

Maria explains her plan for revenge. She will compose a love letter to Malvolio in Olivia's handwriting, so that he will believe that his mistress is in love with him.

Activities

Actors' interpretations (7): Sir Andrew

In the 1996 film, Richard E Grant gained a great deal of audience sympathy in the way in which he said 'I was adored once too.'

1. Discuss whether you think there actually was someone who once loved Sir Andrew, or whether this is simply another example of the way he imitates everybody else.
2. Try performing the line in different ways for different effects.

Plot review (3): the strands

The third strand of the plot – the revenge against Malvolio – is now well under way.

A What exactly is Maria planning to do? Discuss what the letter will say, what she will do with it, and how it will help them to gain their revenge.

B Which aspects of Malvolio's character are being exploited in Maria's plot? What does she say about him, and what evidence is there in his behaviour to support her evaluations?

C Discuss the ways in which Shakespeare is using Malvolio and Feste to link the different plot strands together.

151–152 **obscure epistles of love** vaguely worded love-letters

153 **manner of his gait** the way he walks

155 **feelingly personated** perfectly described

156–158 **on a forgotten matter** *If Maria and Olivia find some writing that they had forgotten about, they have difficulty telling from the handwriting which of them wrote it.*

159–160 **I smell a device ...** I detect a plot.

164 **My purpose is ... a horse ...** That's the general idea.

165–166 **And your horse ...** *Sir Andrew manages one witty pun but Maria's beats it (punning on 'ass' and 'as').*

168 **physic** medicine

171 **observe his construction ...** see what he makes of it

173 **Penthesilea** *was Queen of the Amazons.*

175 **a beagle, true-bred** a small pedigree dog *(a great compliment from a hunting man like Sir Toby).*

177 **I was adored once too** *perhaps the saddest of Sir Andrew's 'me too' contributions*

180 **If I cannot recover ...** If I can't win your niece *(in marriage)* I'm in a real mess *(having wasted all his money).*

MARIA	I will drop in his way some obscure epistles of love; wherein, by the colour of his beard, the shape of his leg, the manner of his gait, the expressure of his eye, forehead, and complexion, he shall find himself most feelingly personated. I can write very like my lady your niece; on a forgotten matter we can hardly make distinction of our hands.
SIR TOBY	Excellent! I smell a device.
SIR ANDREW	I have 't in my nose, too.
SIR TOBY	He shall think, by the letters that thou wilt drop, that they come from my niece, and that she's in love with him.
MARIA	My purpose is, indeed, a horse of that colour.
SIR ANDREW	And your horse now would make him an ass.
MARIA	Ass, I doubt not.
SIR ANDREW	O! 't will be admirable.
MARIA	Sport royal, I warrant you; I know my physic will work with him. I will plant you two, and let the fool make a third, where he shall find the letter; observe his construction of it. For this night, to bed, and dream on the event. Farewell.

Blazon?

155

160

165

170

Exit.

SIR TOBY	Good night, Penthesilea.
SIR ANDREW	Before me, she's a good wench.
SIR TOBY	She's a beagle, true-bred, and one that adores me; what o' that?
SIR ANDREW	I was adored once too.
SIR TOBY	Let's to bed, knight. Thou hadst need send for more money.
SIR ANDREW	If I cannot recover your niece, I am a foul way out.

175

180

2.4 Orsino's palace

Orsino sends for feste to sing him a song that will relieve his heartache.

182	**cut** *a term of abuse: see 2.5.88*
184	**burn some sack** heat up and spice some sherry
184–185	**'t is too late ...** *The scene ends where it began.*
1	**good morrow** good morning
2	**but that piece of song** but only that song
3	**antique** old-fashioned
4	**passion** suffering
5	**light airs** light-hearted tunes
5	**recollected terms** artificial compositions
6	**giddy-pacéd times** *Orsino is in the mood for something traditional, rather than a clever composition which suits the pace of the modern world.*
16	**In the sweet pangs of it** while you are enjoying it and suffering at the same time
17–20	**For such as I am ...** All true lovers are like me, unreliable (**unstaid**) and restless (**skittish**) in all other emotions (**motions**), except those to do with the constant idea (**image**) of the person they love.

SIR TOBY	Send for money, knight; if thou hast her not i' the end, call me cut.
SIR ANDREW	If I do not, never trust me, take it how you will.
SIR TOBY	Come, come; I'll go burn some sack; 't is too late to go to bed now. Come, knight; come knight. 185

Exeunt.

Scene 4

A room in the Duke's palace.

Enter DUKE, VIOLA, CURIO and others.

DUKE	Give me some music. Now, good morrow, friends. Now, good Cesario, but that piece of song, That old and antique song we heard last night; Methought it did relieve my passion much, More than light airs and recollected terms 5 Of these most brisk and giddy-pacéd times. Come; but one verse.
CURIO	He is not here, so please your lordship, that should sing it.
DUKE	Who was it? 10
CURIO	Feste, the jester, my lord; a fool that the lady Olivia's father took much delight in. He is about the house.
DUKE	Seek him out, and play the tune the while.

Exit CURIO.

Music.

Come hither, boy: if ever thou shalt love, 15
In the sweet pangs of it remember me;
For such as I am all true lovers are,
Unstaid and skittish in all motions else
Save in the constant image of the creature
That is beloved. How dost thou like this tune? 20

2.4 Orsino's palace

As Orsino is giving Viola–Cesario advice about love, Feste arrives, and Orsino asks him to sing.

Activities

Character review: Orsino (4)

Look at Orsino's description of himself as a lover (15–20) and discuss the dramatic irony underlying his words.

What is he implying in his image that 'women are as roses' (38–39)? What does that choice of image tell us about him?

Shakespeare's Language (4): verbs and pronouns

A Check that you know what the verbs and pronouns are in the following:
- O, she that hath a heart ...
- I saw your brother ...
- He was a bachelor then

B Looking back at lines 15–46, note down Shakespeare's version of the following:
- if ever you love
- how do you like this tune?
- you speak mastery
- your eye has stayed upon some favour, hasn't it?
- in that way, she wears to him
- however we praise ourselves
- I think it is well
- are used to chanting it

C Find other examples from the play, and then formulate some grammatical rules governing the use of pronouns and the forms of verbs.

21–22 **It gives a very echo ...** It perfectly represents the deepest feelings of love.

22 **Thou dost speak masterly** You talk like an expert.

23–24 **thine eye Hath stayed ...** You have seen a face (**favour**) that you love.

25 **by your favour** if I may say so

26 **Of your complexion** rather like you

30 **so wears she to him** she adapts herself to suit him

31 **So sways she level ...** she always controls her husband's feelings

33 **Our fancies are more giddy** our desires are more changeable

35 **I think it well** I'm sure you're right.

37 **Or thy affection ...** otherwise your desires will not remain strong

39 **Being once displayed** the very hour their beauty has bloomed, it is lost

44 **spinsters** women spinning wool

45 **bones** bobbins *(for lace-making)*

46 **Do use to chant it** often sing it

46 **silly sooth** simple truth

47 **dallies with** dwells lovingly on

48 **Like the old age** as they did in the old days

VIOLA	It gives a very echo to the seat Where Love is throned.
DUKE	Thou dost speak masterly. My life upon 't, young though thou art, thine eye Hath stayed upon some favour that it loves; Hath it not, boy?
VIOLA	A little, by your favour.
DUKE	What kind of woman is 't?
VIOLA	Of your complexion.
DUKE	She is not worth thee, then. What years, i' faith?
VIOLA	About your years, my lord.
DUKE	Too old, by heaven. Let still the woman take An elder than herself, so wears she to him, So sways she level in her husband's heart; For, boy, however we do praise ourselves, Our fancies are more giddy and unfirm, More longing, wavering, sooner lost and worn, Than women's are.
VIOLA	I think it well, my lord.
DUKE	Then let thy love be younger than thyself, Or thy affection cannot hold the bent; For women are as roses, whose fair flower Being once displayed, doth fall that very hour.
VIOLA	And so they are; alas! that they are so; To die, even when they to perfection grow.

Re-enter CURIO and FESTE.

DUKE	O, fellow! come, the song we had last night. Mark it, Cesario; it is old and plain; The spinsters and the knitters in the sun, And the free maids that weave their thread with bones, Do use to chant it; it is silly sooth, And dallies with the innocence of love, Like the old age.

25

30

35

40

45

(handwritten margin note) Couldn't make something up?

2.4 Orsino's palace

Feste sings and is rewarded by Orsino.

Activities

Actors' interpretations (9): animals

Many actors find that it helps to think of their character as a particular animal. Helen Schlesinger, who played Viola in 1997, said: 'One of the things we did in rehearsal was to play Viola as a monkey and Orsino as a lion. It was to do with developing their relationship and also to do with gender.' Philip Voss (Malvolio in the same production) said: 'I also chose an animal for Malvolio. I thought at first a budgerigar because it looks at itself in a mirror, but then I read about Puritans and I've now come up with a giraffe.'

1. Discuss which animals you think might fit your own interpretation of Viola, Orsino and Malvolio and explain why you have chosen them. Which animals might you choose if you were playing Feste, Olivia, Aguecheek or Maria?

2. Make some decisions and then try reading some of a character's speeches with your animal in mind, bringing out some of its characteristics. Choose important moments, such as Malvolio's 2.3 entrance, Orsino's first appearance, or Feste's witty exchange with Olivia in 1.5.

51–52 ***Come away ...*** Come to me, death and lay me in a cypress-wood coffin.

57–58 ***My part of death ...*** I am the truest lover who has ever died for love.

67 **pains** trouble

70–71 **pleasure will be paid ...** We all have to pay for our fun in the end.

72 **Give me now leave ...** *Orsino's polite way of asking Feste to leave.*

73 **melancholy god** *Saturn. (People born under Saturn were supposed to be gloomy.)*

73–75 **and the tailor make thy doublet ...** I hope the tailor makes your suit (**doublet**) out of shot-silk (**taffeta**). *Feste links Orsino with a cloth and a precious stone (***opal***), which are both known for changing their colours in different lights, implying that Orsino himself is changeable in his loves.*

75–79 **I would have ...** Men as constant as that ought to go to sea, which is itself changeable in its moods and would carry them here and there on business as they wished; because that would be a way of making their inconstancy profitable.

FESTE	Are you ready, sir?
DUKE	Ay; prithee, sing.

50

Music.

FESTE   *Come away, come away, death,*
  And in sad cypress let me be laid;
Fly away, fly away, breath;
  I am slain by a fair cruel maid.
My shroud of white, stuck all with yew,
    O! prepare it;
My part of death, no one so true
    Did share it.
Not a flower, not a flower sweet,
  On my black coffin let there be strown;
Not a friend, not a friend greet
  My poor corse, where my bones shall be thrown;
A thousand thousand sighs to save,
    Lay me O! where
Sad true lover never find my grave,
    To weep there.

55

60

65

DUKE   (*Gives him money*) There's for thy pains.

FESTE   No pains, sir; I take pleasure in singing, sir.

DUKE   I'll pay thy pleasure, then.

FESTE   Truly, sir, and pleasure will be paid, one time or   70
another.

DUKE   Give me now leave to leave thee.

FESTE   Now, the melancholy god protect thee, and the
tailor make thy doublet of changeable taffeta, for
thy mind is a very opal! I would have men of   75
such constancy put to sea, that their business
might be everything and their intent everywhere;
for that's it that always makes a good voyage of
nothing. Farewell.

Exit.

DUKE   Let all the rest give place.

2.4 Orsino's palace

Asking Viola–Cesario to go back to Olivia, Orsino claims that no woman could experience a love as strong as his.

Activities

Character review: Orsino (5)

Zoe Wanamaker said: 'Orsino deludes himself; he is blind about women and how they should be treated; supposes that they cannot be spoken to honestly or share the thoughts and feelings of men.'

A List the differences that Orsino claims exist between women and men (32–35; 38–39; and 94–104). Discuss whether or not you agree that such differences exist.

B Discuss what problems Orsino might create if he carries on thinking in this way. How might Viola change him – make him 'grow up'?

C Discuss whether you would agree that Zoe Wanamaker has, in fact, put her finger on Orsino's major deficiency – that he simply does not understand women – or whether, more fundamentally, he fails to understand himself.

81 **yond same sovereign cruelty** that same queen of cruelty

82–85 **my love, more noble ...** My love, more refined than the mass of mankind, isn't interested in (**prizes not**) land. I value (**hold**) the wealth she happens to possess (**parts that fortune hath bestowed upon her**) as lightly (**giddily**) as fortune does itself.

86–87 **But 't is that miracle ...** but what attracts my soul is the miraculous beauty that nature has adorned her with

90 **Say that ...** *Although Viola begins with 'What if there were some lady ...', she is clearly talking about herself.*

94 **sides** body

95 **bide** bear

97 **lack retention** cannot hold so much

99–100 **No motion of the liver ...** *The Elizabethans believed that the liver was the source of passions. Orsino claims that women's love is shallower than men's, and compares it to eating, saying that it is more like a passing appetite. They soon suffer from overeating (**surfeit**), not wanting any more (**cloyment**) and then feeling sick (**revolt**).*

104 **owe** have for

Older man talking to a younger man about love.

Exeunt CURIO and attendants.

| | Once more, Cesario, | 80 |

Get thee to yond same sovereign cruelty;
Tell her, my love, more noble than the world,
Prizes not quantity of dirty lands;
The parts that fortune hath bestowed upon her,
Tell her, I hold as giddily as fortune;   85
But 't is that miracle and queen of gems
That nature pranks her in, attracts my soul.

VIOLA   But if she cannot love you, sir?

DUKE   I cannot be so answered.

VIOLA   Sooth, but you must.
Say that some lady, as perhaps there is,   90
Hath for *your* love as great a pang of heart
As you have for Olivia; you cannot love her;
You tell her so; must she not then be answered?

DUKE   There is no woman's sides
Can bide the beating of so strong a passion   95
As love doth give my heart; no woman's heart
So big, to hold so much; they lack retention.
Alas! their love may be called appetite,
No motion of the liver, but the palate,
That suffer surfeit, cloyment, and revolt;   100
But mine is all as hungry as the sea,
And can digest as much. Make no compare
Between that love a woman can bear me
And that I owe Olivia.

VIOLA   Ay, but I know –

DUKE   What dost thou know?   105

VIOLA   Too well what love women to men may owe;
In faith, they are as true of heart as we.   *← talking about herself*
My father had a daughter loved a man,
As it might be, perhaps, were I a woman,
I should your lordship.

DUKE   And what's her history?   110

neo-platonic
older → younger

Olivia's garden

Orsino does not realise that Viola–Cesario is describing her own love for him. At the beginning of Scene 5, Sir Toby and Sir Andrew are joined by Fabian, who also wants revenge on Malvolio.

Activities

Character review: Viola (3)

In pairs, re-read Viola's conversation with Orsino, looking closely at the way she reacts to his statements and questions.

A What does Viola say about women's love in this conversation?

B 1. Find the moments where (a) Viola avoids answering Orsino's questions directly; or (b) there is dramatic irony, because Orsino understands her reply to mean one thing, while the audience know it to mean another.
2. What do you think she means by 'and yet I know not' (122)?
3. What do these responses reveal about her feelings and attitudes at this point in the play?

C Zoe Wanamaker said: 'At the end of the scene we see Viola, for almost the only time in the play, really depressed.' Discuss whether you agree. What evidence is there in the text which made the actress interpret her in this way? How else might Viola be played at the end of this scene, and how might a very different mood be shown to the audience?

112–113 **But let concealment ...** Keeping the secret caused 'her sister's' rose-coloured (**damask**) cheeks to pale.

114 **with ... melancholy** pale and sickly with misery

115 **like Patience ...** *This figure was often placed on graves to remind people that they had to be patient and put up with grief.*

118 **Our shows are more than will** We show off our love, but it is more than we actually feel.

118–119 **still we prove Much ...** We are always good at making promises, but do not prove our love in our actions.

125 **can give no place, bide no denay** will not give in nor put up with any refusal

1 **Come thy ways** Come on.

2 **scruple** tiny bit

2–3 **let me be boiled to death ...** *Fabian jokes that there's more chance of being boiled in an icy liquid than missing the fun of humiliating Malvolio.*

4 **niggardly** mean

5 **sheep-biter** *Malvolio savages other people for their 'sins'.*

8 **bear-baiting** *Activity in which a bear was tied to a post and tormented by dogs.*

10 **fool him black and blue** bruise him with our trickery

VIOLA	A blank, my lord. She never told her love,
	But let concealment, like a worm i' the bud,
	Feed on her damask cheek, she pined in thought,
	And with a green and yellow melancholy,
constant →	She sat like Patience on a monument, 115
	Smiling at grief. Was not this love indeed?
	We men may say more, swear more; but indeed
	Our shows are more than will, for still we prove
	Much in our vows, but little in our love. *He does not love her*
DUKE	But died thy sister of her love, my boy? 120
VIOLA	I am all the daughters of my father's house,
	And all the brothers too; and yet I know not.
	Sir, shall I to this lady?
DUKE	Ay, that's the theme.
	To her in haste; give her this jewel; say
	My love can give no place, bide no denay. 125

Exeunt.

Scene 5

Olivia's garden.

Enter SIR TOBY BELCH, SIR ANDREW AGUECHEEK and FABIAN.

SIR TOBY	Come thy ways, Signior Fabian.
FABIAN	Nay, I'll come; if I lose a scruple of this sport, let me be boiled to death with melancholy.
SIR TOBY	Would'st thou not be glad to have the niggardly, rascally sheep-biter come by some notable 5 shame?
FABIAN	I would exult, man; you know he brought me out o' favour with my lady about a bear-baiting here.
SIR TOBY	To anger him we'll have the bear again, and we will fool him black and blue; shall we not, Sir 10 Andrew?
SIR ANDREW	An we do not, it is pity of our lives.

2.5 Olivia's garden

Maria tells the three men to hide behind the hedge. She places the letter on the ground and leaves as Malvolio enters, imagining what it would be like to be Count Malvolio.

Activities

Character review: Fabian (1)

A Fabian is not mentioned in the script before his entrance in this scene. Discuss the information Shakespeare gives us about him in the first few lines. What kind of job do you think he does in Olivia's household? Where might he appear earlier in the play, so that the audience can get used to seeing him and not be puzzled by his sudden appearance here?

B As they enter, each of these characters has a particular reason for wanting revenge on Malvolio (and so do Feste and Maria). Discuss what each character's motive is.

C Many people have been puzzled by the entrance of Fabian here. For one thing, we expect to see Feste; for another, it is odd to bring in a completely new character when there does not seem to be a need for one.

1. Look back and find evidence that Feste is expected to appear in this scene.
2. Discuss why Shakespeare might have decided to introduce a new character and thereby keep Feste out of this particular incident.

13–14 metal of India Maria is 'pure gold' in Toby's eyes.

15 box-tree the garden hedge

17–18 practising behaviour posing

20 contemplative idiot He will be made a fool by what he thinks of the letter.

21 Close Keep hidden!

23 tickling This is a cunning way in which to catch trout.

24 'T is but fortune ... Malvolio believes that it is only a matter of chance that he is a steward rather than a lord.

24–27 Malvolio has convinced himself that Maria told him Olivia admired (**did affect**) him and that he has heard Olivia (**herself**) come near to saying that, if she ever fell in love, it would be with someone like him (**of my complexion**).

30 overweening arrogant

31–33 Contemplation ... Thinking about himself conceitedly makes him look like a male turkey. See how he struts around (**jets**) with his uplifted (**advanced**) plumes!

34 'Slight God's light!

40–41 example for 't Malvolio convinces himself that he could marry Olivia, because such a thing has been known to happen before. The **yeoman** was the man who looked after the clothes.

Enter MARIA.

SIR TOBY   Here comes the little villain. How now, my metal
of India?

MARIA   Get ye all three into the box-tree. (*They hide   15
behind the hedge*) Malvolio's coming down this
walk; he has been yonder i' the sun, practising
behaviour to his own shadow this half hour.
Observe him, for the love of mockery; for I know
this letter will make a contemplative idiot of him.   20
Close, in the name of jesting! Lie thou there; (*She
throws down a letter*) for here comes the trout that
must be caught with tickling.

Exit.

Enter MALVOLIO.

MALVOLIO   'T is but fortune; all is fortune. Maria once told
me she did affect me; and I have heard herself   25
come thus near, that, should she fancy, it should
be one of my complexion. Besides, she uses me
with a more exalted respect than any one else that
follows her. What should I think on 't?

SIR TOBY   (*To SIR ANDREW and FABIAN*)
Here's an overweening rogue!   30

FABIAN   O, peace! Contemplation makes a rare turkey-
cock of him; how he jets under his advanced
plumes!

SIR ANDREW   'Slight, I could so beat the rogue!

SIR TOBY   Peace! I say!   35

MALVOLIO   To be Count Malvolio!

SIR TOBY   Ah, rogue!

SIR ANDREW   Pistol him, pistol him.

SIR TOBY   Peace! peace!

MALVOLIO   There is example for 't; the lady of the Strachy   40
married the yeoman of the wardrobe.

I was surprised that maria would help fool malvolio ?

2.5 Olivia's garden

Sir Toby is infuriated by Malvolio's fantasy of being married to Olivia and has to be quietened by Fabian.

Activities

Actors' interpretations (10): the box-tree

'Get ye all three into the box-tree ...'
There have been many different approaches to this scene:

Discuss how else the scene could be staged. Draw a set that would work, showing where the characters hide (remember they have to be visible to the audience when they say their lines); where Malvolio walks around; and where the letter is dropped.

42 **Jezebel** *a woman in the Bible famous for her pride.*

43 **deeply in** absorbed in his thoughts

44 **blows him** swells him up with pride

46 **state** throne

47 **stone-bow** catapult

49 **day-bed** couch

53 **to have the humour of state** to be in the mood for exercising my authority

54 **demure travel of regard** a serious look around at all the people present

55–56 **place** social status, rank.

57 **Bolts and shackles!** *to be placed on Malvolio's legs in prison*

61 **or play with my –** *Perhaps Malvolio is about to say 'my steward's chain' and then remembers that he would no longer be a steward but a rich man.*

64 **with cars** Horses and carts will not drag any sound out of them.

66 **quenching** suppressing

67 **an austere regard of control** a stern authoritarian look

68 **take you a blow ...** punch you in the mouth

71–72 **give me this prerogative ...** allow me to say

SIR ANDREW	Fie on him, Jezebel!
FABIAN	O, peace! now he's deeply in; look how imagination blows him.
MALVOLIO	Having been three months married to her, sitting in my state, –

45

SIR TOBY	O! for a stone-bow, to hit him in the eye.
MALVOLIO	Calling my officers about me, in my branched velvet gown; having come from a day-bed, where I have left Olivia sleeping, –

50

SIR TOBY	Fire and brimstone!
FABIAN	O, peace! peace!
MALVOLIO	And then to have the humour of state; and after a demure travel of regard, telling them I know my place, as I would they should do theirs, to ask for my kinsman Toby, –

55

SIR TOBY	Bolts and shackles!
FABIAN	O, peace, peace, peace! Now, now.
MALVOLIO	Seven of my people, with an obedient start, make out for him. I frown the while, and perchance wind up my watch, or play with my – some rich jewel. Toby approaches, curtsies there to me, –

60

SIR TOBY	Shall this fellow live?
FABIAN	Though our silence be drawn from us with cars, yet peace!

65

MALVOLIO	I extend my hand to him thus, quenching my familiar smile with an austere regard of control –
SIR TOBY	And does not Toby take you a blow o' the lips then?
MALVOLIO	Saying, "Cousin Toby, my fortunes having cast me on your niece, give me this prerogative of speech," –

70

2.5 Olivia's garden

In the middle of his daydream, Malvolio notices the letter and immediately believes the handwriting to be Olivia's.

Activities

Actors' interpretations (11): interjections

Much of the comedy in this scene comes from the way Sir Toby and the others keep interjecting comments in between Malvolio's speeches.

A List some of the insults and exclamations that Toby, Andrew and Fabian utter from behind the box-tree.

B Act out lines 24–85, bringing out Sir Toby's anger, Sir Andrew's stupidity and Fabian's attempts to restrain the two.

C Discuss what aspects of Malvolio their interjections focus upon and how they make you feel about the unaware steward. (Refer back to your feelings about Malvolio at the end of 2.3.)

Shakespeare's language (5): bawdy

Quite a bit of Shakespeare's comedy involves some pretty crude (or 'bawdy') jokes.

Check the notes to make sure you understand the source of Shakespeare's bawdy humour in lines 87–91 and then act out the extract, showing how, in their different ways, neither Malvolio nor Sir Andrew understands the joke.

---

74 **amend your drunkenness** stop being a drunkard

75 **scab!** a common insult

76 **break the sinews of our plot** ruin our plan

82 **employment** business

84 *The* **woodcock** *was well known for its stupidity.*

84 **gin** trap

85–86 **the spirit of humours ...** *Sir Toby prays that whatever it is that influences people's actions should suggest that Malvolio reads out loud.*

88–91 **her very *C's* ...** *Malvolio is being made to look ridiculous, reading out C, U and T (which make up 'cut', a slang term for the female genitalia), while* **makes she her great *P's*** *means 'urinates'. Sir Andrew misses the joke.*

89–90 **in contempt of question** without any doubt

93 **By your leave, wax** *He asks the wax seal for permission to break it.*

94 **Soft!** Wait a minute!

94 **the impressure her Lucrece** The imprint is of her sealing-ring, which bears the figure of Lucretia *(a Roman heroine; see line 107).*

97 **liver and all** with total passion

2.5

SIR TOBY	What, what?
MALVOLIO	"You must amend your drunkenness."
SIR TOBY	Out, scab!
FABIAN	Nay, patience, or we break the sinews of our plot.
MALVOLIO	"Besides, you waste the treasure of your time with a foolish knight," –
SIR ANDREW	That's me, I warrant you.
MALVOLIO	"One Sir Andrew," –
SIR ANDREW	I knew 't was I; for many do call me fool.
MALVOLIO	(*Seeing the letter on the ground*) What employment have we here?
FABIAN	Now is the woodcock near the gin.
SIR TOBY	O, peace! and the spirit of humours intimate reading aloud to him!
MALVOLIO	(*Picking up the letter*) By my life, this is my lady's hand! These be her very *C*'s, her *U*'s, and her *T*'s; and thus makes she her great *P*'s. It is, in contempt of question, her hand.
SIR ANDREW	Her *C*'s, her *U*'s, and her *T*'s; why that?
MALVOLIO	(*Reading*) *To the unknown beloved, this, and my good wishes*: Her very phrases! By your leave, wax. (*He opens the letter*) Soft! and the impressure her Lucrece, with which she uses to seal; 't is my lady. To whom should this be?
FABIAN	This wins him, liver and all.
MALVOLIO	(*Reading*) *Jove knows I love;* *But who?* *Lips, do not move:* *No man must know.*

75

80

85

90

95

100

2.5 Olivia's garden

Malvolio struggles to work out Maria's cleverly constructed riddles and find some meaning in the letter that relates to him.

Activities

Shakespeare's language (6): imagery

Shakespeare's audience would have been very familiar with activities such as hunting with hounds or hawking, and would understand all the jargon.

A Many of the expressions we use today originally had something to do with hunting. Discuss the meanings and the origins of the following:
- you're on the wrong track
- you're barking up the wrong tree
- you're getting warm
- we're keeping it at bay
- that's our quarry
- the press are hounding her.

B Re-read lines 115–128 and check the notes which go with the following images:
- with what wing the staniel checks at it (115)
- he is now at a cold scent (123)
- Sowter will cry upon 't ... though it be as rank as a fox (124–125)
- the cur is excellent at faults (127–128).

Then pick one image and draw a cartoon featuring Malvolio in the place of the animal being described (for example, sniffing out a scent like a hound). How far do these images match your own picture of Malvolio's behaviour and character?

(Continued on page 82)

103 **number's altered** the form of the verse has changed

105 **brock** badger *(well known for stinking)*

107 ***But silence ...*** Silence stabs my heart, like the knife that Lucretia used to kill herself.

110 **fustian** overdone *(and therefore perfect for Malvolio)*

114 **dressed** prepared for

115 *A* **staniel** *is a kestrel, which turns in flight (***checks***) when it spies its prey.*

118 **evident to ...** perfectly clear to anyone of normal intelligence

120 **... portend** What meaning is there behind the positioning of the letters?

123 **at a cold scent** He has lost the scent.

124–125 **Sowter ...** *A common name for a hound, which thinks it's clever to have found the scent, even though it's as strong as a fox's.*

127–128 The dog (**cur**) is excellent at picking up cold scents (**faults**).

129–130 **no consonancy in the sequel ...** What follows doesn't fit. It falls apart (**suffers**) when you examine it closely (**under probation**).

132 **And *O* shall end** *Malvolio will end in a hangman's noose.*

"No man must know." What follows? The
number's altered! "No man must know." If this
should be thee, Malvolio?

SIR TOBY   Marry, hang thee, brock!   105

MALVOLIO   (*Reading*)
       I may command where I adore;
      But silence, like a Lucrece knife,
      With bloodless stroke my heart doth gore:
      M, O, A, I, doth sway my life.

FABIAN   A fustian riddle!   110

SIR TOBY   Excellent wench, say I.

MALVOLIO   "M, O, A, I, doth sway my life." Nay, but first, let
me see, let me see, let me see.

FABIAN   What a dish o' poison has she dressed him!

SIR TOBY   And with what wing the staniel checks at it!   115

MALVOLIO   "I may command where I adore." Why, she may
command me; I serve her; she is my lady. Why,
this is evident to any formal capacity; there is no
obstruction in this. And the end, – What should
that alphabetical position portend? If I could   120
make that resemble something in me, – Softly!
M, O, A, I, –

SIR TOBY   O! ay, make up that; he is now at a cold scent.

FABIAN   Sowter will cry upon 't, for all this, though it be as
rank as a fox.   125

MALVOLIO   M, Malvolio; M, why, that begins my name!

FABIAN   Did not I say he would work it out? the cur is
excellent at faults.

MALVOLIO   M, – but then there is no consonancy in the
sequel; that suffers under probation; A should   130
follow, but O does.

FABIAN   And O shall end, I hope.

2.5 Olivia's garden

Malvolio reads on. The letter advises him to behave like a great man, rather than a steward, and to wear yellow, cross gartered stockings. He is now convinced that it is a love letter from Olivia.

Activities

C Make a note of the images used here and jot down what effect they have in helping to describe, not only Malvolio's behaviour, but the attitude of the others to it.

Add your notes to an imagery database and discuss what contribution the imagery has made to your understanding of characters and themes.

Character review: Malvolio (2)

Philip Voss (Malvolio in 1997) said: 'I find the Puritan angle affecting all rehearsals: it's a brilliant parody [mockery of Puritans' attitudes and behaviour]. He is a Puritan in his thinking but when he goes into his fantasy it's not to do good in the world, it's not to help anybody, it's to wear velvet gowns and to have rich jewels and to order people about.'

Draw up two lists: (a) of all the things that Puritans were against (see page 211); and (b) all the things that appear to be part of Malvolio's 'fantasy' hopes. Think about:

- the relationship he would like to have with Sir Toby and the others
- the relationship he would like to have with Olivia
- the social status he would like to enjoy.

136 **detraction at your heels** misfortune following you

138 **this simulation is not ...** this part of the puzzle is different

142 *revolve* think about it

147 *inure* get yourself used to

147–148 *cast thy humble slough* throw off your humility

148 *opposite* argumentative

149–150 *tang arguments of state* speak out on serious subjects

150–151 *put thyself into the trick of singularity* behave eccentrically

157 *would alter services with thee* would love to change positions with you. *(If Olivia married him, he would have authority over her.)*

159 **champain** flat, open country

160–161 **politic authors** clever writers

161 **baffle** treat him rudely

162 **point-devise ...** exactly

163 **jade** deceive

164 **every reason excites** every argument persuades me

167 **manifests ...** shows clearly

168–169 **drives me ...** encourages me to wear these clothes she likes

170 **strange, stout** distant, proud

171–172 **even with the swiftness ...** as fast as I can put them on

SIR TOBY	Ay, or I'll cudgel him, and make him cry O!
MALVOLIO	And then *I* comes behind.
FABIAN	Ay, an you had any eye behind you, you might see more detraction at your heels than fortunes before you.

SIR TOBY   Ay, or I'll cudgel him, and make him cry O!

MALVOLIO   And then *I* comes behind.

FABIAN   Ay, an you had any eye behind you, you might see   135
more detraction at your heels than fortunes
before you.

MALVOLIO   *M, O, A, I*; this simulation is not as the former;
and yet, to crush this a little, it would bow to me,
for every one of these letters are in my name.   140
Soft! here follows prose.

*(Reading) If this fall into thy hand, revolve! In my
stars I am above thee; but be not afraid of greatness;
some are born great, some achieve greatness, and some
have greatness thrust upon them. Thy Fates open their   145
hands; let thy blood and spirit embrace them, and to
inure thyself to what thou art like to be, cast thy
humble slough and appear fresh. Be opposite wih a
kinsman, surly with servants; let thy tongue tang
arguments of state; put thyself into the trick of   150
singularity: she thus advises thee that sighs for thee.
Remember who commended thy yellow stockings, and
wished to see thee ever cross-gartered; I say, remember.
Go to, thou art made if thou desirest to be so; if not,
let me see thee a steward still, the fellow of servants,   155
and not worthy to touch Fortune's fingers. Farewell.
She that would alter services with thee,*
                    THE FORTUNATE-UNHAPPY

Daylight and champain discovers not more; this
is open. I will be proud, I will read politic   160
authors, I will baffle Sir Toby, I will wash off gross
acquaintance, I will be point-devise the very man.
I do not now fool myself, to let imagination jade
me; for every reason excites to this, that my lady
loves me. She did commend my yellow stockings   165
of late; she did praise my leg being cross-gartered;
and in this she manifests herself to my love, and
with a kind of injunction drives me to these
habits of her liking. I thank my stars I am happy. I
will be strange, stout, in yellow stockings, and   170
cross-gartered, even with the swiftness of putting

2.5 Olivia's garden

Malvolio leaves, vowing to follow the letter's instructions and smile when he is next in Olivia's presence. The conspirators are overjoyed and lavish praise on Maria when she returns.

Activities

Actors' interpretations (12): comedy

A Many actors have made a great deal of Malvolio's attempts to force his serious features into a smile.

Rehearse his exit yourself and compare your performance with other people's in a 'Malvolio's smile' competition, to see who can come up with the most hideous effort.

B Maria has composed the letter so cleverly that Malvolio takes some time to realise (a) that it is addressed to him; and (b) what it is saying.

Look back through lines 82–179 and annotate the script, showing the steps by which Malvolio gradually understands the full meaning of the letter. (You might add notes such as 'still puzzled here' . . . 'starts to realise that it's composed as a riddle' . . .). Then act out the scene, bringing out his gradual realisation. You may wish to make a convincing 'prop' letter for Malvolio to read from.

C Write a short essay on the different potential sources of comedy in this scene and the means by which actors might bring it out. The main headings might be 'situation comedy', 'visual comedy', 'verbal comedy' and 'comedy of character'.

175 **entertainest** If you accept

176 **thy smile becomes thee well** Smiling really suits you.

181 **Sophy** the (*very rich*) Shah of Persia

182 **device** plot

184–185 *Another joke like this one would suffice as the payment* (**dowry**) *from the bride's family.*

187 **gull-catcher** idiot-catcher

188 **set thy foot . . .** as a conqueror might do

190–191 **play my freedom . . .** Shall I gamble with my freedom in a game of dice (**tray-trip**) and become bound to you as your slave?

194 **when the image of it leaves him** when he wakes up

197 **aqua-vitae** alcoholic spirits

on. Jove and my stars be praised! Here is yet a
postscript.

(Reading) Thou canst not choose but know who I am.
If thou entertainest my love, let it appear in thy   175
smiling; thy smile becomes thee well; therefore in my
presence still smile, dear my sweet, I prithee.

Jove, I thank thee. I will smile; I will do every
thing that thou wilt have me.

Exit.

FABIAN	I will not give my part of this sport for a pension	180
	of thousands to be paid from the Sophy.	

SIR TOBY   I could marry this wench for this device.

SIR ANDREW   So could I too.

SIR TOBY   And ask no other dowry with her but such another
jest.   185

SIR ANDREW   Nor I neither.

FABIAN   Here comes my noble gull-catcher.

Re-enter MARIA.

SIR TOBY   Wilt thou set thy foot o' my neck?

SIR ANDREW   Or o' mine either?

SIR TOBY   Shall I play my freedom at tray-trip, and become   190
thy bond-slave?

SIR ANDREW   I' faith, or I either?

SIR TOBY   Why, thou hast put him in such a dream, that
when the image of it leaves him he must run
mad.   195

MARIA   Nay, but say true; does it work upon him?

SIR TOBY   Like aqua-vitae with a midwife.

Olivia's garden

Sir Toby, Sir Andrew and Fabian enthusiastically follow Maria off to watch what happens when Malvolio next approaches Olivia.

Activities

Character review: Sir Andrew (2)

'I'll make one, too . . .' (209) Sir Andrew doesn't have much imagination or wit and often cannot come up with anything more original than 'Me too!'

Perform lines 180 to the end of the scene in different ways, first trying to derive humour from Sir Andrew's pathetic attempts to be one of the gang, and then playing him for sympathy. Which works best, in terms of the way you see Sir Andrew in the play as a whole?

Character review: Viola (4)

Imagine you are Viola. Write down your thoughts and the confusion you feel as you leave Orsino to make your second visit to Olivia.

You could begin: How on earth is all this going to sort itself out . . .?

Before you begin to write consider Viola's feelings about:
* Olivia's 'returning' the ring, and your concern for her feelings
* your love for Orsino
* Orsino's views on the difference between women's love and men's
* the story you told Orsino about your 'father's daughter'.

201 **abhors** detests

205 **notable contempt** famous figure of fun

207 **Tartar** Tartarus *(the hell in Greek mythology)*

209 **I'll make one too** *This is almost like 'Can I join in?'*

MARIA   If you will then see the fruits of the sport, mark
             his first approach before my lady; he will come to
             her in yellow stockings, and 't is a colour she   200
             abhors; and cross-gartered, a fashion she detests;
             and he will smile upon her, which will now be so
             unsuitable to her disposition, being addicted to a
             melancholy as she is, that it cannot but turn him
             into a notable contempt. If you will see it, follow   205
             me.

SIR TOBY   To the gates of Tartar, thou most excellent devil of
             wit.

SIR ANDREW   I'll make one too.

                                                           Exeunt.

Exam practice

Character review: Malvolio (3)

1. Read the section on page 211 to find out exactly what Puritans believed in, and particularly what they disapproved of. Find out why Malvolio would dislike Sir Toby's behaviour so much.
2. As Malvolio exits, he threatens Maria that Olivia 'shall know of it, by this hand'.

A Make a list of the things that Malvolio might report to Olivia in order to get Maria into trouble.

B In pairs, improvise the report that Malvolio gives to Olivia (remembering to use his own language and mannerisms) and react as you think Olivia might.

C Assume that Malvolio does not want to omit a single detail of his account of these misdemeanours, and therefore decides to make an official report in writing. Create his official report, writing in a style appropriate to the character. (Re-read his speeches to confirm your ideas about the style in which he might write.)

John Woodvine as Malvolio

Actors' interpretations (13): the letter

A To work convincingly, the letter has to be written on both sides of the paper and at particular angles.

Donald Sinden as Malvolio

Re-read lines 87–177 and discuss how the various sections of the letter should be arranged on the paper to make it work for the actor reading it and the audience watching. Then make a rough version, but don't write out the whole script.

B Imagine you are directing a performance of *Twelfth Night*. Annotate 2.5.82–179 to help the actor playing Malvolio to perform the scene effectively. Give advice on:
- movements and actions;
- how to speak the lines;
- where to pause;
- facial expressions;
- how Malvolio is feeling.

C Write an analysis of the steps by which Malvolio interprets the letter (2.5.82–179) and is taken in by it. For each step, give you opinions on the particular feature of Malvolio's character (for example, his 'self-love') which seems to be his undoing.

Character review: relationships

Draw up two diagrams: (a) showing who is in love with whom at the end of Act 2; (b) predicting which characters will finally be paired off, and how it will come about in each case.

3.1 Olivia's garden

Viola–Cesario meets Feste and, after some clever wordplay, he talks about the way words can mean different things.

Shakespeare's language (7): wordplay

The first 42 lines of this scene provide many examples of wordplay. This section of dialogue is actually about words and the ways in which they can be made to mean different things.

A Look back to pages 10 and 12 to remind yourself about double meanings and the ways in which they are used for humour. Find the statements from Feste which mean:

- somebody who is clever with words can turn meanings inside-out
- a person's 'word' these days is no longer good enough: we have to sign contracts
- because words can have different meanings, it is impossible to prove anything with them.

B Find and explain the wordplay which depends upon different meanings of:

- 'live by'
- 'lie by'
- 'dally with'
- 'care for'.

What does this wordplay add to your understanding of Feste and the kind of character he is?

(Continued on page 92)

1–2 **... live by thy tabor?** Do you make a living out of playing the drum?

3 *Feste deliberately picks up the other meaning of 'live by'.*

8 **So thou mayest say** You might as well say. *(Viola is not to be outdone by Feste's wordplay.)*

8 **lies by** has sex with

9 **stands by** is supported financially by

11–12 **You have said ...** Absolutely right! What an age we live in! A wise saying (**sentence**) is nothing more than a kid leather (**cheveril**) glove to a clever person.

14 **dally nicely** play cleverly *(and also 'play around' in the sexual sense)*

15 **wanton** sexually promiscuous

16 **I would therefore** In that case, I wish

20–21 **words are very rascals ...** A person's 'word' is no longer any good: these days we have to sign a contract (**bond**).

24–25 **loath to prove reason ...** I'm reluctant to prove a logical argument using words.

26 **I warrant** I'm sure

Act 3

Scene 1

Olivia's garden.

Enter VIOLA and FESTE with a tabor.

VIOLA	Save thee, friend, and thy music. Dost thou live by thy tabor?
FESTE	No, sir, I live by the church.
VIOLA	Art thou a churchman?
FESTE	No such matter, sir; I do live by the church, for I do live at my house, and my house doth stand by the church.
VIOLA	So thou mayest say, the king lies by a beggar if a beggar dwell near him; or, the church stands by thy tabor, if thy tabor stand by the church.
FESTE	You have said, sir. To see this age! A sentence is but a cheveril glove to a good wit; how quickly the wrong side may be turned outward!
VIOLA	Nay, that's certain; they that dally nicely with words may quickly make them wanton.
FESTE	I would therefore my sister had had no name, sir,
VIOLA	Why, man?
FESTE	Why, sir, her name's a word; and to dally with that word might make my sister wanton. But indeed words are very rascals since bonds disgraced them.
VIOLA	Thy reason, man?
FESTE	Troth, sir, I can yield you none without words; and words are grown so false, I am loath to prove reason with them.
VIOLA	I warrant thou art a merry fellow, and carest for nothing.

Marginal notes: 5 — fool joking around

Line numbers: 5, 10, 15, 20, 25

91

3.1 Olivia's garden

Describing himself as Olivia's 'corrupter of words', Feste begs money off Viola–Cesario.

Activities

C Discuss Feste's play on the expression 'care for' (lines 28–31). What do you think lies behind his comment 'I do not care for you'? Discuss the following possibilities:

- he means that he does not like Cesario (because 'he' is as sharp-witted as Feste himself)
- he actually knows that Cesario is a young woman in disguise (as Ben Kingsley did in the 1996 film) and does not like the deception
- he simply means that it is not his responsibility according to his 'conscience' to 'take care of' Cesario.

How might each of these meanings fit your overall interpretation of Feste?

Feste also says, 'I do care for something'. Stephen Boxer (Feste in 1997) took the view that 'There is one person for whom he will do anything and that is Olivia. She's his bread and butter, but . . . the line "I do care for something" . . . to me indicates the possibility that he cares for Olivia, perhaps loves her.'

Can you find any clues in the script which support Stephen Boxer's interpretation?

30 **I would** I wish

35 **pilchards** small herrings

38 **late** recently

39 **orb** world

40–42 **the fool should be . . .** (1) I would like to be with Orsino as often as with Olivia; (2) there's as much foolishness in Orsino's house as in Olivia's . . . I think I saw you there?

43 **pass upon** if you're having a go at me *(a fencing term)*

45 **Now Jove . . .** Now, when Jove gets his next delivery of hair

52 **put to use** invested to gain interest

53–57 *In the Trojan war,* **Pandarus** *acted as go-between for his niece* **Cressida** *and the warrior* **Troilus**. *Cressida ended up a beggar.*

58 **construe** explain

| FESTE | Not so, sir; I do care for something; but in my conscience, sir, I do not care for you; if that be to care for nothing, sir, I would it would make you invisible. | 30 |

| VIOLA | Art not thou the Lady Olivia's fool? | |

| FESTE | No, indeed, sir; the Lady Olivia has no folly; she will keep no fool, sir, till she be married; and fools are as like husbands as pilchards are to herrings – the husband's the bigger. I am indeed not her fool, but her corrupter of words. | 35 |

| VIOLA | I saw thee late at the Count Orsino's. | |

| FESTE | Foolery, sir, does walk about the orb like the sun; it shines everywhere. I would be sorry, sir, but the fool should be as oft with your master as with my mistress. I think I saw your wisdom there. | 40 |

| VIOLA | Nay, an thou pass upon me, I'll no more with thee. Hold, there's expenses for thee. | |

Gives him a piece of money.

| FESTE | Now Jove, in his next commodity of hair, send thee a beard! | 45 |

| VIOLA | By my troth, I'll tell thee, I am almost sick for one, *(aside)* though I would not have it grow on *my* chin. Is thy lady within? | |

| FESTE | (*Looking at the money*) Would not a pair of these have bred, sir? | 50 |

| VIOLA | Yes, being kept together and put to use. | |

| FESTE | I would play Lord Pandarus of Phrygia, sir, to bring a Cressida to this Troilus. | |

| VIOLA | I understand you, sir; 't is well begged. | 55 |

| FESTE | The matter, I hope, is not great, sir, begging but a beggar; Cressida was a beggar. My lady is within, sir. I will construe to them whence you come; who you are and what you would are out of my |

3.1 Olivia's garden

Viola considers how fools like Feste need to be wise. Sir Toby and Sir Andrew enter, followed by Olivia and Maria.

Activities

Actors' interpretations (14): fools and wit

In praising Feste's abilities, Viola remarks that a successful fool has to observe the people he is making jokes about, understand them and concentrate upon their particular qualities.

A Re-read Viola's words (62–70) in pairs, dividing the speech at regular points so that it sounds like a conversation. What are the key points Viola makes?

B Discuss modern comedians who, in your opinion, have this ability, and give examples of the kinds of things they do. Which of them would make an interesting Feste?

C 'A sentence is but a cheveril glove to a good wit; how quickly the wrong side may be turned outward!' (11–13) Discuss the link between the ambiguities of language in the play and the ambiguities of character and behaviour.

60–61 *In avoiding the cliché 'element', Feste chooses* **welkin,** *which literally means 'sky'.*

63 **craves** demands, requires

65 **The quality ... and the time** know their social status and pick the right moment

66–67 **Not, like the haggard ...** Not, like an untrained hawk. *(A good fool must be selective and not simply take every opportunity to make a joke.)*

68 **labour ...** It takes as much hard work as any profession.

69–70 **For folly ...** It is appropriate for him to display his well-chosen foolery; but intelligent people who behave foolishly ruin their reputations for cleverness.

73 ***Dieu ...*** God save you, sir.

74–75 ***Et vous ...*** And you too; I am your servant. *(Sir Andrew's reply suggests that he might have used up all the French he knows.)*

76–79 *Sir Toby is being too formal and ceremonious here with words such as* **encounter, desirous** *and* **trade.** *Viola gives as good as she gets, picking up the 'trading' language and playing with words.*

80 **Taste** Try out

81 **under-stand** *a pun: her legs stand under her*

85 **gait** walking

	welkin; I might say "element", but the word is overworn.	60

Exit.

VIOLA	This fellow's wise enough to play the fool,	
	And to do that well craves a kind of wit;	
	He must observe their mood on whom he jests,	
	The quality of persons, and the time,	65
	Not, like the haggard, check at every feather	
	That comes before his eye. This is a practice	
	As full of labour as a wise man's art,	
	For folly that he wisely shows is fit;	
	But wise men, folly-fall'n, quite taint their wit.	70

Enter SIR TOBY BELCH and SIR ANDREW AGUECHEEK.

SIR TOBY	Save you, gentleman.	

VIOLA	And you, sir.	

SIR ANDREW	*Dieu vous garde, monsieur.*	

VIOLA	*Et vous aussi; votre serviteur.*	

SIR ANDREW	I hope, sir, you are; and I am yours.	75

SIR TOBY	Will you encounter the house? My niece is desirous you should enter, if your trade be to her.	

VIOLA	I am bound to your niece, sir; I mean, she is the list of my voyage.	

SIR TOBY	Taste your legs, sir; put them to motion.	80

VIOLA	My legs do better under-stand me, sir, than I understand what you mean by bidding me taste my legs.	

SIR TOBY	I mean, to go, sir, to enter.	

VIOLA	I will answer you with gait and entrance. But we are prevented.	85

Enter OLIVIA and MARIA.

3.1 Olivia's garden

Sir Andrew is impressed by Viola–Cesario's courtly language. Olivia asks to talk with Viola–Cesario in private and repeats that she does not want to hear any more mention of Orsino.

Activities

Themes (5): appearance and reality

In giving her name as Cesario, Viola continues the pretence of being a young man.

A As a class, discuss how far it is possible to judge by appearances. Then brainstorm other sayings or proverbs (All that glisters . . .), or even complete stories (Red Riding Hood . . .), which get across the moral that you should not judge by appearances.

B Brainstorm other examples (a) from stories, films or television; and (b) from Acts 1 and 2 of *Twelfth Night*, of people appearing to be what they aren't (or disguising what they really are). What similarities are there between their behaviour and Viola's?

C Add to your theme database by beginning a list, headed 'The Theme of Appearance and Reality', and continue to add to it as the play progresses. To start off your list, look back at:
- 1.2.45–49 and 51–54
- 1.4.30–34 and 41–42
- 1.5.31–34 and 55–57
and then find examples in Act 2.

89 **rare courtier** *Sir Andrew is impressed that Cesario has all the social skills learned at court.*

91–92 **My matter hath no voice . . .** My business is only to be discussed with you, who will listen in a receptive (**pregnant**) way, having kindly granted (**vouchsafed**) me an audience (**ear**).

101–102 **'T was never merry world . . .** In the old days people did not pay compliments by pretending to be humble.

104 **his** his servant

107 **blanks** empty *(like blank sheets of paper, or coins before they have been stamped)*

108 **whet** sharpen up *(to make her more interested in Orsino)*

109–114 **by your leave** *Olivia politely refuses to hear about Orsino and then asks permission to talk about her feelings for Cesario.*

111 **undertake another suit** woo on behalf of someone else *(himself!)*

112 **solicit** present the case for

113 **spheres** *The planets and stars were thought to be in spheres around the earth; as they revolved, they made beautiful music which humans could not hear.*

(*To* OLIVIA) Most excellent accomplished lady, the
heavens rain odours on you!

SIR ANDREW That youth's a rare courtier. "Rain odours!" –
Well.   90

VIOLA My matter hath no voice, lady, but to your own
most pregnant and vouchsafed ear.

SIR ANDREW "Odours", "pregnant", and "vouchsafed"; I'll get
'em all three all ready.

OLIVIA Let the garden door be shut, and leave me to my   95
hearing.

                        Exeunt SIR TOBY, SIR ANDREW and MARIA.

(*To* VIOLA) Give me your hand, sir.

VIOLA My duty, madam, and most humble service.

OLIVIA What is your name?

VIOLA Cesario is your servant's name, fair princess.   100

OLIVIA *My* servant, sir! 'T was never merry world
Since lowly feigning was called compliment.
You're servant to the Count Orsino, youth.

VIOLA And he is yours, and his must needs be yours;
Your servant's servant is your servant, madam.   105

OLIVIA For him, I think not on him; for his thoughts,
Would they were blanks rather than filled with me!

VIOLA Madam, I come to whet your gentle thoughts
On his behalf.

OLIVIA   O! by your leave, I pray you,
I bade you never speak again of him;   110
But, would you undertake another suit,
I had rather hear you to solicit that
Than music from the spheres.

VIOLA   Dear lady, –

3.1 Olivia's garden

Olivia apologises for having sent a ring after Viola–Cesario and wonders what 'he' must think of her. Viola says that she pities Olivia.

115 **enchantment** *Olivia thinks that Cesario has bewitched her.*

116 **abuse** treat wrongly

118 **Under your hard construction** You must think very badly of me.

121–123 **Have you not set ...** *Olivia thinks of her honour as being like a bear, tied to the stake; the* **unmuzzled** *dogs baiting it are the critical opinions of Olivia held by Cesario.*

124 **To one of your receiving** To someone as sensitive as you

125 **A cypress ...** My feelings are hidden from you only by a thin veil (which shows that I am in mourning).

128 **grize** step; **for 't is a vulgar proof that** it happens all the time that

130 **time to smile** *If her love is hopeless, she had better accept the fact cheerfully.*

132–133 **be a prey ...** *Olivia feels that at least she has fallen for 'a king among men'.*

134 **upbraids** criticises

135 **I will not have you** I can't force you to marry me.

136 **is come to harvest** is mature

138 **westward-ho!** *The cry of the Thames watermen.*

139 **Grace and good disposition** God bless you and give you peace of mind.

OLIVIA	Give me leave, beseech you. I did send,
	After the last enchantment you did here, 115
	A ring in chase of you; so did I abuse
	Myself, my servant, and, I fear me, you;
	Under your hard construction must I sit,
	To force that on you, in a shameful cunning,
	Which you knew none of yours, what might you
	think? 120
	Have you not set mine honour at the stake,
	And baited it with all the unmuzzled thoughts
	That tyrannous heart can think?
	To one of your receiving, enough is shown;
	A cypress, not a bosom, hides my heart. 125
	So, let me hear you speak.
VIOLA	I pity you.
OLIVIA	That's a degree to love.
VIOLA	No, not a grize; for 't is a vulgar proof
	That very oft we pity enemies.
OLIVIA	Why, then, methinks 't is time to smile again. 130
	O world! how apt the poor are to be proud.
	If one should be a prey, how much the better
	To fall before the lion than the wolf!

Clock strikes.

	The clock upbraids me with the waste of time.
	Be not afraid, good youth, I will not have you; 135
	And yet, when wit and youth is come to harvest,
	Your wife is like to reap a proper man.
	There lies your way, due west.
VIOLA	Then westward-ho!
	Grace and good disposition attend your ladyship!
	You'll nothing, madam, to my lord by me? 140
OLIVIA	Stay;
	I prithee, tell me what thou think'st of me.
VIOLA	That you do think you are not what you are.
OLIVIA	If I think so, I think the same of you.

[Handwritten annotations: "better be turned down by some one cute than an ugly wolf"; "graceful"]

3.2 Olivia's house

Olivia openly declares her love for Viola–Cesario, who replies that she will never give her heart to any woman, and leaves with Olivia's request for 'him' to visit her again. As Scene 2 opens, Sir Andrew declares that he is leaving as Olivia is plainly not interested in him.

Activities

Shakespeare's language (9): dramatic irony and ambiguity

Bearing in mind the fact that Viola/Cesario was originally played by a boy, think about how many different ways Shakespeare's audience might understand Viola's statement 'I am not what I am' (145).

1. Discuss the meanings
   - that Olivia would understand, thinking she is speaking to a young man called Cesario
   - that a modern audience would understand, remembering that Cesario is actually Viola (and knowing Viola's history)
   - that Shakespeare's audience would understand, knowing that Viola was being acted by a boy.
2. When a statement can have more than one meaning, we say it is ambiguous, and talk about ambiguity. Discuss the ambiguity in the following lines of Viola's:
   - I am all ... brothers too (2.4.121–122)
   - By my troth ... *my* chin (3.1.47–48)
   - I have one ... woman has (3.1.162–163).

---

146 **I would you were** ... I wish you were what I would like you to be.

149–150 **O! what a deal of scorn** ... O! doesn't he look beautiful when he's scornful, contemptuous and angry!

151–152 **A murderous guilt** ... A murderer can more easily hide his guilt, than a lover his feelings.

154 **maidhood** virginity

155 **maugre** in spite of

156 **Nor wit nor reason** neither intelligence nor common sense

157–159 **Do not extort** ... Don't use the fact that I am wooing you as a reason for not wooing me. But rather overcome (**fetter**) that argument with this one.

166 **deplore** speak sorrowfully

167–168 **for thou perhaps may'st move** ... You might perhaps persuade the heart that hates Orsino's love, to like it.

1 **jot** moment. *(Sir Andrew feels that he doesn't stand a chance with Olivia, having seen her reaction to Cesario.)*

2 **venom** poison *(referring to Sir Andrew's 'deadly' resolve)*

VIOLA	Then think you right; I am not what I am.	145
OLIVIA	I would you were as I would have you be!	
VIOLA	Would it be better, madam, than I am? I wish it might, for now I am your fool.	
OLIVIA	(*Aside*) O! what a deal of scorn looks beautiful In the contempt and anger of his lip.	150
	A murderous guilt shows not itself more soon	
	Than love that would seem hid; love's night is noon.	
	(*To* VIOLA) Cesario, by the roses of the spring,	
	By maidhood, honour, truth, and every thing,	
	I love thee so, that, maugre all thy pride,	155
	Nor wit nor reason can my passion hide.	
	Do not extort thy reasons from this clause,	
	For that I woo, thou therefore hast no cause;	
	But rather reason thus with reason fetter,	
	Love sought is good, but given unsought is better.	160
VIOLA	By innocence I swear, and by my youth,	
	I have one heart, one bosom, and one truth,	
	And that no woman has; nor never none	
	Shall mistress be of it, save I alone.	
	And so adieu, good madam; never more	165
	Will I my master's tears to you deplore.	
OLIVIA	Yet come again, for thou perhaps may'st move That heart, which now abhors, to like his love.	

Exeunt.

Scene 2

A room in Olivia's house.

Enter SIR TOBY BELCH, SIR ANDREW AGUECHEEK and FABIAN.

SIR ANDREW	No, faith, I'll not stay a jot longer.
SIR TOBY	Thy reason, dear venom; give thy reason.
FABIAN	You must needs yield your reason, Sir Andrew.
SIR ANDREW	Marry, I saw your niece do more favours to the

3.2 Olivia's house

Sir Toby and Fabian persuade Sir Andrew that Olivia deliberately showed favour to Cesario in order to spur Sir Andrew into action.

Activities

Shakespeare's language (10): persuasion

A As the scene begins, Sir Andrew is determined to leave. What is his main reason for wanting to leave? What arguments do Sir Toby and Fabian use in persuading him to stay?

B Annotate lines 1–30, showing what might be going through Sir Andrew's head, as he changes from being determined to leave, to agreeing to challenge Cesario. Then put your books down and improvise the scene, up to Sir Andrew's exit (51).

C Look at other moments in the play where characters engage in persuasion (either openly, such as Viola in 1.2 & 1.5; Orsino in 1.4 & 2.4; Olivia in 1.5 & 3.2; Antonio in 2.1; or more subtly, as with Sir Toby in 1.3; Feste in 1.5; and the letter in 2.5). Consider in each case who is persuading whom to do what, and by what means. Make notes and then write a short essay on 'The importance of persuasion to the action of *Twelfth Night*'.

11 **'Slight** God's light!

14 **grand-jurymen** Judgement and reason (*personified*) have seen a lot of legal cases.

17 **dormouse** Fabian means 'dormant' (sleeping); but, given how timid Sir Andrew is, he has hit upon an appropriate word!

22–23 **This was looked for ...** Olivia expected you to do this and you 'copped out'.

23–24 **the double gilt of ...** You missed this golden opportunity

24–27 **you are now sailed** To convince him that Olivia now looks upon him 'coldly' Fabian uses two images: (1) of someone sailing to the cold northern seas; and (2) of an icicle hanging from the beard of the famous Dutch explorer William Barentz.

27–28 **unless you do redeem it ...** unless you put it right by some praiseworthy deed of courage or clever plotting

30 **I had as lief ...** I'd as gladly be a Puritan as an underhand plotter.

31 **build me thy fortunes ...** base your hopes of success

34–37 **there is no love-broker ...** Nothing persuades a woman to love a man better than stories of his courage.

102

	count's serving-man than ever she bestowed upon me; I saw 't i' the orchard.	5
SIR TOBY	Did she see thee the while, old boy? Tell me that.	
SIR ANDREW	As plain as I see you now.	
FABIAN	This was a great argument of love in her toward you.	10
SIR ANDREW	'Slight! will you make an ass o' me?	
FABIAN	I will prove it legitimate, sir, upon the oaths of judgement and reason.	
SIR TOBY	And they have been grand-jurymen since before Noah was a sailor.	15
FABIAN	She did show favour to the youth in your sight only to exasperate you, to awake your dormouse valour, to put fire in your heart, and brimstone in your liver. You should then have accosted her, and with some excellent jests, fire-new from the mint, you should have banged the youth into dumbness. This was looked for at your hand, and this was balked; the double gilt of this opportunity you let time wash off, and you are now sailed into the north of my lady's opinion, where you will hang like an icicle on a Dutchman's beard, unless you do redeem it by some laudable attempt, either of valour or policy.	20

25 |
SIR ANDREW	An 't be any way, it must be with valour, for policy I hate; I had as lief be a Brownist as a politician.	30
SIR TOBY	Why then, build me thy fortunes upon the basis of valour; challenge me the count's youth to fight with him; hurt him in eleven places; my niece shall take note of it; and assure thyself, there is no love-broker in the world can more prevail in man's commendation with woman than report of valour.	35
FABIAN	There is no way but this, Sir Andrew.	

3.2 Olivia's house

Shortly after Sir Andrew has gone away to write a challenge to Cesario, Maria enters with news that Malvolio is behaving hilariously.

Activities

Shakespeare's language (11): forms of address

'If thou thou'st him ...' (43) – the personal pronouns for 'you' were different in Shakespeare's day. The general rules were 'thou' was used when:
- addressing a friend
- addressing someone below you in status
- speaking rudely to someone.

'You' (sometimes 'ye') was used when:
- addressing someone you did not know well
- addressing someone higher in status
- addressing more than one person.

(Continued on page 106)

40–44 **in a martial hand** Write it aggressively! Be fierce (**curst**) and to the point (**brief**), well expressed and original (**full of invention**). Insult him in writing (**with the licence of ink**). It won't be a mistake (**amiss**) to call him 'thou' two or three times.

44 **as many lies ...** Accuse him of being a liar.

46 **bed of Ware** *a bed famous for its great size*

47 **gall** (1) bitterness; (2) *ink was made from oak-galls (growths)*

48 **goose-pen** *The goose was thought to be cowardly.*

51 ***cubiculo*** your bedroom

52 **dear manakin to you** puppet that you enjoy controlling

59 **hale** pull

63–64 And the face (**visage**) of his opponent (**opposite**) doesn't suggest (**bears ... no great presage**) that he's violent!

66 **If you desire the spleen** If you want a good laugh.

67 **Yond gull** That idiot

67–68 **is turned heathen, a very renegado** *Malvolio has given up his religion and turned against being a Puritan.*

68–70 **for there is no Christian ...** No Christian, who wants to be saved through their belief, could ever believe such gross impossibilities!

SIR ANDREW	Will either of you bear me a challenge to him?
SIR TOBY	Go, write it in a martial hand; be curst and brief; 40

SIR TOBY   Go, write it in a martial hand; be curst and brief;   40
it is no matter how witty, so it be eloquent and
full of invention; taunt him with the licence of
ink; if thou thou'st him some thrice, it shall not
be amiss; and as many lies as will lie in thy sheet
of paper, although the sheet were big enough for   45
the bed of Ware in England, set 'em down; go,
about it. Let there be gall enough in thy ink,
though thou write with a goose-pen, no matter;
about it.

SIR ANDREW   Where shall I find you?   50

SIR TOBY   We'll call thee at the *cubiculo*; go.

Exit SIR ANDREW.

FABIAN   This is a dear manakin to you, Sir Toby.

SIR TOBY   I have been dear to him, lad; some two thousand
strong or so.

FABIAN   We shall have a rare letter from him; but you'll   55
not deliver it?

SIR TOBY   Never trust me, then; and by all means stir on the
youth to an answer. I think oxen and wainropes
cannot hale them together. For Andrew, if he were
opened, and you find so much blood in his liver   60
as will clog the foot of a flea, I'll eat the rest of the
anatomy.

FABIAN   And his opposite, the youth, bears in his visage
no great presage of cruelty.

Enter MARIA.

SIR TOBY   Look, where the youngest wren of nine comes.   65

MARIA   If you desire the spleen, and will laugh yourselves
into stitches, follow me. Yond gull Malvolio is
turned heathen, a very renegado; for there is no
Christian, that means to be saved by believing

3.3 A street in Illyria

Because of his love for Sebastian, Antonio has followed him to offer his protection.

Activities

1. Match up these quotations with the characters who said them and explain why they used 'you' or 'thou' in each case:
   (a) you are like to be much advanced (1.4.2)
   (b) Thou know'st no less but all (1.4.13)
   (c) tell me where thou hast been (1.5.1)
   (d) My masters, are you mad . . .? (2.3.83)
   (e) Dost thou think, because thou art virtuous . . .? (2.3.110–111)
   (f) But if she cannot love you, sir? (2.4.88)

   (Valentine; Cesario; Sir Toby; Orsino; Maria; Malvolio)

2. Explain Sir Toby's suggestion 'if thou thou'st him' (3.2.43).

3. Thee, thy and thine: look at the following phrases and discuss in what ways 'thee', 'thy' and 'thine' are used to indicate status or relationship:
   • I thank thee (1.2.62)
   • To call his fortune thine (1.4.40)
   • give thy reason (3.2.2)
   • We'll call thee at the *cubiculo* (3.2.51)

73 **villainously** awfully

73 **like a pedant** like a schoolmaster *(in other words, badly dressed!)*

74 **dogged him** followed him

77–78 **new map** *A new world map had been produced in 1599 and included the East Indies. Malvolio's 'laughter lines' are compared with the map's navigation lines.*

79 **forbear** stop myself from

1 **by my will** willingly

2 **since you make your pleasure . . .** since you seem to enjoy taking trouble

4 **stay behind you** let you go on without me

4 **desire** love

6–9 **And not all love . . .** I wasn't only motivated by a desire to see you – though that would have been enough to send me on a longer journey – but by an anxiety (**jealousy**) about what might happen to (**befall**) you, since you are unfamiliar with (**skilless in**) this country.

15–18 **and oft good turns . . .** People often repay good turns with such valueless things as 'Thank yous'. But if I were as wealthy as I am honest (**were my worth, as is my conscience, firm**), you would be rewarded properly (**find better dealing**).

rightly, can ever believe such impossible passages   70
of grossness. He's in yellow stockings!

SIR TOBY   And cross-gartered?

MARIA   Most villainously; like a pedant that keeps a
school i' the church. I have dogged him like his
murderer. He does obey every point of the letter   75
that I dropped to betray him; he does smile his
face into more lines than is in the new map with
the augmentation of the Indies. You have not
seen such a thing as 't is; I can hardly forbear
hurling things at him. I know my lady will strike   80
him; if she do, he'll smile and take 't for a great
favour.

SIR TOBY   Come, bring us, bring us where he is.

                                                    Exeunt.

Scene 3

A street.

Enter SEBASTIAN and ANTONIO.

SEBASTIAN   I would not by my will have troubled you;
But since you make your pleasure of your pains,
I will no further chide you.

ANTONIO   I could not stay behind you; my desire,
More sharp than filéd steel, did spur me forth;   5
And not all love to see you, though so much
As might have drawn one to a longer voyage,
But jealousy what might befall your travel,
Being skilless in these parts, which to a stranger,
Unguided and unfriended, often prove   10
Rough and unhospitable; my willing love,
The rather by these arguments of fear,
Set forth in your pursuit.

SEBASTIAN   My kind Antonio,
I can no other answer make but thanks,
And thanks, and ever thanks; and oft good turns   15

3.3 A street in Illyria

Sebastian wants to do some sightseeing, but Antonio is reluctant to accompany him as he is a wanted man in Illyria, having once fought against Orsino's galleys. He lends Sebastian his purse and they arrange to meet at the Elephant.

Activities

Character review: Antonio (2)

A Turn back to 2.1 and remind yourself who Antonio is and what his connection is to Viola's brother Sebastian. Discuss exactly why it is that Antonio might be arrested if found in Illyria. Then draw up either a 'Wanted' poster, or the file held on him in police headquarters. (For additional information about his past exploits, look ahead to what Orsino and an officer say about him in 5.1.47–61.)

B What impression have you formed of Antonio from these two scenes (2.1 and 3.3)? Give each of the following qualities a mark out of five, according to how strongly you see it represented in Antonio's behaviour or his past history: generosity; friendship; love; impetuosity (hot-headedness); physical courage; hospitality; anxiety; practical common sense; obstinacy (pig-headedness). Compare your gradings with other people's and discuss the differences.

C Write brief notes on Antonio's contribution to the play so far. Why has Shakespeare included him? What would be missing were he to be removed altogether? Which plot-strand is he related to? Keep your notes for a piece of written work to be completed later.

19 **relics** old buildings, ruins

24 **renown this city** make this city famous

24 **Would you'd pardon me** You'll have to excuse me.

26 **the count his** the count's

27 **I did some service – of such note** I fought so successfully

28 **ta'en** arrested

28 **it would scarce be answered** Nothing I could do would make up for it.

29 **Belike** presumably, I suppose

31–32 **Albeit the quality . . .** Even though the nature of the dispute might well have led to bloodshed.

34 **for traffic's sake** to maintain good relations for trading

35 **stood out** refused

36 **lapséd** caught

37 **open** publicly

39 **the Elephant** *a common inn sign at that time*

40 **bespeak our diet** order some food

41 **beguile** pass

42 **there shall you have me** that's where you'll find me

44 **toy** trinket

45–46 **your store . . .** your own savings should not be spent on trivial things (**idle markets**)

47 **purse-bearer** treasurer

Are shuffled off with such uncurrent pay;
But, were my worth, as is my conscience, firm,
You should find better dealing. What's to do?
Shall we go see the relics of this town?

ANTONIO   Tomorrow, sir; best first go see your lodging.   20

SEBASTIAN I am not weary, and 't is long to night.
I pray you, let us satisfy our eyes
With the memorials and the things of fame
That do renown this city.

ANTONIO   Would you'd pardon me;
I do not without danger walk these streets;   25
Once, in a sea-fight 'gainst the count his galleys,
I did some service – of such note, indeed,
That were I ta'en here it would scarce be answered.

SEBASTIAN Belike you slew great number of his people.

ANTONIO   The offence is not of such a bloody nature,   30
Albeit the quality of the time and quarrel
Might well have given us bloody argument.
It might have since been answered in repaying
What we took from them; which, for traffic's sake,
Most of our city did; only myself stood out;   35
For which, if I be lapséd in this place,
I shall pay dear.

SEBASTIAN   Do not then walk too open.

ANTONIO   It doth not fit me. Hold, sir; here's my purse.
In the south suburbs, at the Elephant,
Is best to lodge; I will bespeak our diet,   40
Whiles you beguile the time and feed your
    knowledge
With viewing of the town; there shall you have me.

SEBASTIAN Why *I* your purse?

ANTONIO   Haply your eye shall light upon some toy
You have desire to purchase; and your store,   45
I think, is not for idle markets, sir.

SEBASTIAN I'll be your purse-bearer, and leave you for an hour.

3.4 Olivia's garden

When Olivia calls for Malvolio, he enters smiling and wearing yellow stockings, cross-gartered.

Activities

Actors' interpretations (15): Malvolio

Malvolio's arrival on stage, wearing yellow stockings and cross-gartered, can be a hilarious moment.

A Look at the three production photographs on page 112, which show what Malvolio can look like while he is still trying to appear a Puritan. Discuss the ways in which each of the three has changed his costume for the entrance in 3.4.

B Decide what your own ideal Malvolio would look like at this point. Which actor would you cast in the role? What kind of costume would he wear in Acts 1 and 2? What would the yellow stockings and cross-gartering look like in this scene?

C Write a description and review, either of one of the Malvolios on video (Alec McCowan, Richard Briers or Nigel Hawthorne), or of a stage performance that you have seen. Give an account of the actor's appearance and stage performance and say how successful the effect was, in your opinion. Try to watch two or more video versions and compare the interpretations of Malvolio.

(Continued on page 112)

2 **feast ...** How shall I entertain him? What shall I give (**bestow of**) him?

3 **youth is bought ...** Young people are more often won over by gifts, than by pleading with them or making promises.

5 **sad and civil** serious and dignified

6 **suits well ...** he fits my mood perfectly

9 **possessed** mad. *(Mentally ill people were thought to be possessed by devils. Notice all the references to the devil by Sir Toby and the others when they meet Malvolio.)*

13 **tainted in 's wits** his mind is 'contaminated'

14–15 **I am as mad ...** *Malvolio's madness is 'merry' (since he does nothing but smile); hers is sad (for the love of Cesario).*

18 **upon a sad occasion** about a serious business

19 **sad** *Malvolio means (1) serious; and (2) suffering from melancholy, caused by the jaundice resulting from the obstruction of the cross-gartering.*

ANTONIO	To the Elephant.
SEBASTIAN	I do remember.

Exeunt.

Scene 4

Olivia's garden.

Enter OLIVIA and MARIA.

OLIVIA	I have sent after him; he says he'll come,	
	How shall I feast him, what bestow of him?	
	For youth is bought more oft than begged or	
	borrowed.	
	I speak too loud.	
	Where is Malvolio? He is sad and civil,	5
	And suits well for a servant with my fortunes;	
	Where is Malvolio?	
MARIA	He's coming, madam; but in very strange manner.	
	He is, sure, possessed, madam.	
OLIVIA	Why, what's the matter? Does he rave?	10
MARIA	No, madam; he does nothing but smile; your	
	ladyship were best to have some guard about you	
	if he come, for sure the man is tainted in 's wits.	
OLIVIA	Go call him hither.	

Exit MARIA.

	I am as mad as he,	
	If sad and merry madness equal be.	15

Re-enter MARIA with MALVOLIO.

	How now, Malvolio!	
MALVOLIO	Sweet lady, ho, ho.	
OLIVIA	Smilest thou? I sent for thee upon a sad occasion.	
MALVOLIO	Sad, lady! I could be sad; this does make some	

3.4 Olivia's garden

Olivia is amazed by Malvolio's behaviour and is totally mystified when he quotes from the letter.

Activities

22–23 **Please one ...** If it pleases you, it pleases everybody *(a line from a popular song)*

26 **black** sad *(black being the colour of melancholy)*

27 **It** the letter

28–29 **Roman hand** italic handwriting

30 **go to bed** *Olivia thinks that he needs a lie down; he completely misunderstands her!*

35 **At your request ...** I will speak to you if you wish. Yes *(sarcastically)*, nightingales *(attractive songbirds)* answer jackdaws *(common, noisy scavengers).*

38 **'Be not afraid ...'** *Malvolio reminds Olivia of what she supposedly wrote.*

45 **restore thee** bring back your sanity

	obstruction in the blood, this cross-gartering; but what of that? If it please the eye of one, it is with me as the very true sonnet is, "Please one, and please all".	20
OLIVIA	Why, how dost thou, man? What is the matter with thee?	25
MALVOLIO	Not black in my mind, though yellow in my legs. It did come to his hands, and commands shall be executed; I think we do know the sweet Roman hand.	
OLIVIA	Wilt thou go to bed, Malvolio?	30
MALVOLIO	To bed! ay, sweetheart, and I'll come to thee.	
OLIVIA	God comfort thee! Why dost thou smile so, and kiss thy hand so oft?	
MARIA	How do you, Malvolio?	
MALVOLIO	At your request! Yes; nightingales answer daws.	35
MARIA	Why appear you with this ridiculous boldness before my lady?	
MALVOLIO	"Be not afraid of greatness"; 't was well writ.	
OLIVIA	What meanest thou by that, Malvolio?	
MALVOLIO	"Some are born great," –	40
OLIVIA	Ha!	
MALVOLIO	"Some achieve greatness," –	
OLIVIA	What sayest thou?	
MALVOLIO	"And some have greatness thrust upon them."	
OLIVIA	Heaven restore thee!	45
MALVOLIO	"Remember who commended thy yellow stockings" –	
OLIVIA	Thy yellow stockings!	

3.4 Olivia's garden

Thinking that Malvolio must be mad, Olivia gives order that he should be taken care of. Left alone Malvolio begins to interpret Olivia's words and behaviour as confirmation that she loves him.

Activities

Actors' interpretations (16): Malvolio and Olivia

Rehearse lines 1–62 and then annotate the text, to show how each character should behave (see page 00 for an example). Then rehearse the scene again and act it out:

• Olivia: first worrying how she should behave when Cesario arrives, then being taken aback by Malvolio's appearance and behaviour

• Malvolio: trying desperately to behave as directed in the letter, convinced that Olivia loves him

• the servant: totally unprepared to find the very sober and puritanical steward acting in this way.

54 **midsummer madness** *It was believed that people behaved strangely in midsummer.*

56–57 **hardly entreat him back** I had difficulty keeping him out.

59 **looked to** taken care of

62 **miscarry** come to harm

62 **dowry** *the money which will one day go to her husband*

63 **do you come near me now?** Do you begin to understand me?

66 **stubborn** rude

66 **incites** encourages

67–70 **'Cast thy humble ...'** *quotations from the letter. See 2.5.142–157.*

72 **reverend carriage** dignified way of walking

72 **slow tongue** thoughtful way of speaking

72–73 **in the habit ...** in the dress and behaviour of an important person (**some sir of note**)

74 **limed** caught *(as though with sticky bird-lime)*

77 **nor after my degree** and she didn't refer to me by my rank, but called me 'fellow' *(which he takes to mean her equal)*

77–79 **everything adheres together** It all fits! There is not even the tiniest part of a doubt (***dram*** and ***scruple*** *were both small measurements).*

MALVOLIO	"And wished to see thee cross-gartered."	
OLIVIA	Cross-gartered!	50
MALVOLIO	"Go to, thou art made, if thou desirest to be so;" –	
OLIVIA	Am I made?	
MALVOLIO	"If not, let me see thee a servant still."	
OLIVIA	Why, this is very midsummer madness.	

Enter SERVANT.

| SERVANT | Madam, the young gentleman of the Count Orsino's is returned. I could hardly entreat him back; he attends your ladyship's pleasure. | 55 |
| OLIVIA | I'll come to him. | |

Exit SERVANT.

Good Maria, let this fellow be looked to. Where's
my cousin Toby? Let some of my people have a   60
special care of him; I would not have him
miscarry for the half of my dowry.

Exeunt OLIVIA and MARIA.

MALVOLIO   O, ho! do you come near me now? No worse man
than Sir Toby to look to me! This concurs directly
with the letter; she sends him on purpose that I   65
may appear stubborn to him; for she incites me
to that in the letter. "Cast thy humble slough,"
says she; "be opposite with a kinsman, surly with
sevants; let thy tongue tang with arguments of
state; put thyself into the trick of singularity"; and   70
consequently sets down the manner how: as, a
sad face, a reverend carriage, a slow tongue, in the
habit of some sir of note, and so forth. I have
limed her; but it is Jove's doing, and Jove make
me thankful! And when she went away now, "Let   75
this fellow be looked to"; fellow! not Malvolio,
nor after my degree, but fellow. Why, everything
adheres together, that no dram of a scruple, no

3.4 Olivia's garden

When Maria re-enters with Sir Toby and Fabian they treat Malvolio as though he were mad and possessed by the devil.

Activities

Themes (6): madness

Olivia puts Malvolio's odd behaviour down to 'very midsummer madness' (3.4.54) and Sir Toby and the others behave as though he is 'possessed' (86). Look through 3.4.84–144 and list all the references to religion and the devil. Discuss what those references tell us about (a) attitudes to madness in Shakespeare's time; and (b) beliefs about how to cure it.

Shakespeare's Language (12): changing meanings

Update your glossary of changing meanings, to include words such as: hither (2.2.3); pains (2.2.5); fadge (2.2.32); betimes (2.3.2); leman (2.3.26); welkin (2.3.57); politicians (2.3.72); device (2.3.159); physic (2.3.168); complexion (2.4.26); owe (2.4.104); soft (2.5.94); late (3.1.38); welkin (3.1.60); maugre (3.1.155); as lief (3.2.30); belike (3.3.29).

Remember to divide them into (a) words which have a different meaning in Shakespeare's time, and (b) words which no longer exist.

79–80 no incredulous or unsafe circumstance There is nothing about this which is unbelievable or which cannot be depended upon.

82 full prospect total fulfilment

84 sanctity holiness. *(Sir Toby and the others pretend to believe that Malvolio is possessed by the devil.)*

85 drawn in little dragged into a small space *(Malvolio's body)*

85 Legion *the name given to the many devils which possessed a man in the Bible*

90 my private my privacy, my own company

92 Lo, how hollow ... Listen to the deep voice of the devil inside him!

96 Go to Be careful!

97 let me alone leave this to me

98 defy the devil *'Possessed' people sometimes tried to reject (**defy**) the devil publicly.*

101–102 La you! ... Look at that! See how offended he gets if (**an**) you insult the devil!

104 Carry his water ... *A **wise woman** was someone who claimed to diagnose illnesses, often by looking at the patient's urine (**water**).*

106 My lady ... *Notice how Maria keeps referring to Olivia's supposed concern for Malvolio.*

scruple of a scruple, no obstacle, no incredulous
or unsafe circumstance – What can be said?   80
Nothing that can be can come between me and
the full prospect of my hopes. Well, Jove, not I, is
the doer of this, and he is to be thanked.

Re-enter MARIA, with SIR TOBY BELCH and FABIAN.

SIR TOBY	Which way is he, in the name of sanctity? If all the devils of hell be drawn in little, and Legion 85 himself possessed him, yet I'll speak to him.
FABIAN	Here he is, here he is. (*To MALVOLIO*) How is 't with you, sir?
SIR TOBY	How is 't with you, man?
MALVOLIO	Go off; I discard you; let me enjoy my private; go 90 off.
MARIA	Lo, how hollow the fiend speaks within him! Did not I tell you? Sir Toby, my lady prays you to have a care of him.
MALVOLIO	Ah ha! does she so? 95
SIR TOBY	Go to, go to; peace! peace! We must deal gently with him; let me alone. How do you, Malvolio? How is 't with you? What, man! defy the devil; consider, he's an enemy to mankind.
MALVOLIO	Do you know what you say? 100
MARIA	(*To SIR TOBY and FABIAN*) La you! an you speak ill of the devil, how he takes it at heart. Pray God, he be not bewitched!
FABIAN	Carry his water to the wise woman.
MARIA	Marry, and it shall be done tomorrow morning if I 105 live. My lady would not lose him for more than I'll say.
MALVOLIO	How now, mistress!
MARIA	O Lord!

3.4 Olivia's garden

Following the instructions in the letter, Malvolio continues to treat Sir Toby insultingly, and then leaves them. They plot to carry on treating him as though he were mad.

Activities

Actors interpretations (17): 'If this were played upon a stage ...'

Of course, it *is* being played upon a stage, and it *is* improbable. Re-read the part of the scene in which Fabian makes the comment (84–144) and discuss the following possible effects of that line on an audience, saying how far you agree with each one:

- It makes us laugh, because it reminds us how silly the story is.
- It makes us more willing to accept the story as real, because Shakespeare has admitted that it's unlikely.
- It makes us stand back from the story and think about it more.

What other effects might it have?

---

111 **move him** make him angry

115–118 **bawcock ...** *affectionate nicknames. Bawcock is 'fine fellow';* **chuck** *and* **Biddy** *both mean 'chicken'.*

118–119 **'t is not for gravity ...** It's not right for a sensible person to mess around with the devil (**cherry-pit** *was a children's game*).

120 **foul collier** dirty coalman. *(Coalmen were linked with the devil because they were covered in black soot and were believed to be dishonest.)*

123 **minx** *a common term for an immoral and impudent woman*

124 **warrant** promise

126 **I am not of your element** I do not belong to your world.

131–132 **very genius** Even his guardian angel has fallen for the trick (**taken the infection of the device**).

133–134 **pursue him ...** Follow him, to keep the trick going. Otherwise (**lest**), like food left out in the air, it will 'go off' (**take air, and taint**).

135 **make him mad indeed** We will really make him mad.

137 **dark room** *This was the standard treatment to cure madness.*

138 **bound** tied up

SIR TOBY	Prithee, hold thy peace; this is not the way; do you not see you move him? Let me alone with him.	110
FABIAN	No way but gentleness; gently, gently; the fiend is rough, and will not be roughly used.	
SIR TOBY	Why, how now, my bawcock! how dost thou, chuck?	115
MALVOLIO	Sir!	
SIR TOBY	Ay, Biddy, come with me. What, man! 't is not for gravity to play at cherry-pit with Satan; hang him, foul collier!	120
MARIA	Get him to say his prayers, good Sir Toby; get him to pray.	
MALVOLIO	My prayers, minx!	
MARIA	No, I warrant you, he will not hear of godliness.	
MALVOLIO	Go, hang yourselves all! You are idle, shallow things; I am not of your element. You shall know more hereafter.	125

Exit.

SIR TOBY	Is 't possible?	
FABIAN	If this were played upon a stage now, I could condemn it as an improbable fiction.	130
SIR TOBY	His very genius hath taken the infection of the device, man.	
MARIA	Nay, pursue him now, lest the device take air, and taint.	
FABIAN	Why, we shall make him mad indeed.	135
MARIA	The house will be the quieter.	
SIR TOBY	Come, we'll have him in a dark room, and bound. My niece is already in the belief that he's	

3.4 Olivia's garden

Sir Andrew comes back with the challenge that he has written to Cesario. It is a ridiculous piece of writing, but Sir Toby and Fabian pretend to admire it.

Activities

Character review: Malvolio (4)

Having followed the comedy of the trick against Malvolio this far, what would you like to see happen to him before the story ends? How do you feel about the practical joke now? As a class, discuss each of the following possibilities, and then put them in rank order, according to how much you approve of each one.

(a) Malvolio will find out quickly that the letter is a fake and will quietly go back to his role as steward;

(b) he will be imprisoned 'in a dark room and bound' but let out after an hour or so;

(c) he will be imprisoned and only released after Feste has had a chance to mock him;

(d) the whole experience will make Malvolio go 'mad indeed' (i.e. genuinely mad);

(e) he will be so humiliated by the whole business, that he will be forced to leave Olivia's employment;

(f) Olivia will find out what has happened and throw Sir Toby and Sir Andrew out of the house;

(g) (your own suggestion).

139–140 carry it thus ... keep up the joke, for our amusement and his punishment

142 bring the device to the bar bring this trick before the courts to be judged

145 More matter for a May morning More holiday fun!

146 I warrant I guarantee, I promise you

147 vinegar and pepper The letter will be sharply worded and angry.

148 saucy *Another example of the characters' love of wordplay.*

149 do but read Just read it!

151 scurvy fellow *a common insult with no exact meaning today*

152 valiant brave

153 admire *means the same as wonder*

155–156 A good note ... Well said! *That sentence means that he can't have the law on you! (Several of Fabian's comments are along these lines.)*

160–161 sense-less *It is senseless because he has just ruled out the only reason he could have for challenging Cesario – that he is a rival for Olivia's love.*

166 o' the windy side ... You're still on the right side of the law.

mad; we may carry it thus, for our pleasure and
his penance, till our very pastime, tired out of   140
breath, prompt us to have mercy on him; at
which time we will bring the device to the bar,
and crown thee for a finder of madmen. But see,
but see.

Enter SIR ANDREW AGUECHEEK.

FABIAN   More matter for a May morning.   145

SIR ANDREW   Here's the challenge; read it; I warrant there's
vinegar and pepper in 't.

FABIAN   Is 't so saucy?

SIR ANDREW   Ay, is 't, I warrant him; do but read.

SIR TOBY   Give me. (*Takes the letter and reads*) *Youth,*   150
whatsoever thou art, thou art but a scurvy fellow.

FABIAN   Good and valiant.

SIR TOBY   *Wonder not, nor admire not in thy mind, why I do*
call thee so, for I will show thee no reason for 't.

FABIAN   A good note, that keeps you from the blow of the   155
law.

SIR TOBY   *Thou comest to the Lady Olivia, and in my sight she*
uses thee kindly; but thou liest in thy throat; that is
not the matter I challenge thee for.

FABIAN   Very brief, and to exceeding good sense (*Aside*)-   160
less.

SIR TOBY   *I will waylay thee going home; where, if it be thy*
chance to kill me, –

FABIAN   Good.

SIR TOBY   *Thou killest me like a rogue and a villain.*   165

FABIAN   Still you keep o' the windy side of the law; good.

SIR TOBY   *Fare thee well; and God have mercy upon one of our*

3.4 Olivia's garden

When Sir Andrew goes off to lie in wait for Cesario, Sir Toby explains to Fabian that he will not deliver Sir Andrew's letter, but will tell Cesario of the challenge himself. He aims to make the two dualists terrified of each other.

Activities

Shakespeare's language (13): Thou and you

Sir Andrew's challenge certainly follows the rule that you use 'thou' if you want to insult someone or show that they are inferior.

1. Look through the wording to see how many times Sir Andrew repeats the use of 'thou', as though rubbing it in.
2. Remind yourself how the following address each other (and discuss why):
   • Valentine and Cesario in 1.4
   • Orsino and Cesario in 1.4
   • Feste and Olivia in 1.5
   • Olivia and Cesario in 1.5.170–291
   • Olivia addressing Cesario in her imagination in 1.5.294–296
   • Antonio and Sebastian in 2.1
   • Fabian and Sir Andrew in 2.5
   • Sir Toby and Sir Andrew in 2.5

168 **He may have mercy upon mine** ... 'I hope I will be allowed to survive'.

174 **very fit occasion** a perfect opportunity

175 **commerce** conversation

177 **scout me** keep a look out

178 **bum-baily** a sheriff's officer *(who lay in wait to arrest people)*

180–183 **it comes to pass oft** ... It's often the case that if you swear in a boastful way, people think you're more of a man than they would by looking at your actions.

186–188 **gives him out to be** ... shows that he is sensible and refined (**of good capacity and breeding**); and that is confirmed by the fact that Orsino uses him as a messenger to Olivia

191 **clodpole** blockhead

192–193 **set upon Aguecheek** ... make out that Aguecheek has a reputation for courageous deeds

194–195 **as I know his youth** ... As he is young, he will be likely (**apt**) to believe it.

198 **cockatrices** *mythical serpents which could kill by looking at you*

199–200 **give them way** ... Keep out of their way until he leaves, then follow him straightaway.

souls! He may have mercy upon mine, but my hope is
better; and so look to thyself. Thy friend, as thou usest
him, and thy sworn enemy. 170

ANDREW AGUECHEEK

If this letter move him not, his legs cannot, I'll
give 't him.

MARIA   You may have very fit occasion for 't; he is now in
some commerce with my lady, and will by and by   175
depart.

SIR TOBY   Go, Sir Andrew; scout me for him at the corner of
the orchard, like a bum-baily; so soon as ever
thou seest him, draw; and, as thou drawest, swear
horrible; for it comes to pass oft that a terrible   180
oath, with a swaggering accent sharply twanged
off, gives manhood more approbation than ever
proof itself would have earned him. Away!

SIR ANDREW   Nay, let me alone for swearing.

Exit.

SIR TOBY   Now will not I deliver his letter; for the behaviour   185
of the young gentleman gives him out to be of
good capacity and breeding; his employment
between his lord and my niece confirms no less;
therefore this letter, being so excellently ignorant,
will breed no terror in the youth; he will find it   190
comes from a clodpole. But, sir, I will deliver his
challenge by word of mouth; set upon Aguecheek
a notable report of valour; and drive the
gentleman, as I know his youth will aptly receive
it, into a most hideous opinion of his rage, skill,   195
fury, and impetuosity. This will so fright them
both that they will kill one another by the look,
like cockatrices.

FABIAN   Here he comes with your niece; give them way till
he take leave, and presently after him.   200

SIR TOBY   I will meditate the while upon some horrid
message for a challenge.

3.4 Olivia's garden

Olivia declares her love for Viola–Cesario and gives 'him' her picture to wear. As she leaves, Sir Toby approaches and tells Viola–Cesario that a dangerous enemy is waiting for him.

Activities

Character review: Sir Andrew (3)

1. Discuss how this scene adds to your impression of the character: think about (a) what the wording of the challenge reveals of his lack of intelligence; and (b) how the others are treating him. Do you have any sympathy for him at this point?

2. Look back at the earlier reviews on Sir Andrew Aguecheek and consider his actions here. Then write notes on the features of his behaviour and character which make him the archetypal 'gull' of Renaissance comedy (a rich but stupid character, easily fooled and cheated by cleverer, dishonest people pretending to be his friends). Think about:
   - his appearance
   - his motives for being in the household
   - his meeting with Maria (1.3)
   - his problems with language
   - his response to Viola/Cesario's greeting of Olivia (3.1)
   - the ease with which Sir Toby and Fabian manage to persuade him to stay on
   - the challenge
   - the way Toby usually treats him.

   In your opinion, is he more than merely a stock figure of fun?

204 **And laid mine honour ...** I have been too impetuous (**unchary**) in offering my honour like a sacrifice. *(By 'honour', Olivia means, not only her word, but her reputation and even her virginity.)*

205–207 **There's something in me ...** There's something in me that makes me blame myself, but my weakness (**fault**) is so confident (**headstrong**) and powerful (**potent**) that it laughs at any attempt to criticise it (**reproof**).

208–209 **With the same 'haviour ...** My master's suffering is the same as yours.

210 **jewel** *perhaps a brooch with Olivia's portrait in it*

211 **vex** annoy

213–214 **What shall you ask ...** *Olivia would give 'him' anything except her chastity.*

217 **acquit you** release you from your promises to me

222 **That defence thou hast ...** Whatever you are carrying to protect yourself with, use it now!

224–225 Your pursuer (**thy intercepter**), full of anger (**despite**) ... is waiting for you (**attends thee**).

226–227 **Dismount thy tuck** Draw your sword, get ready quickly (**be yare ...**).

Exeunt SIR TOBY, FABIAN and MARIA.

Re-enter OLIVIA, with VIOLA.

OLIVIA	I have said too much unto a heart of stone,
	And laid mine honour too unchary on 't;
	There's something in me that reproves my fault,

205

	But such a headstrong potent fault it is
	That it but mocks reproof.

VIOLA	With the same 'haviour that your passion bears,
	Goes on my master's grief.

OLIVIA	Here; wear this jewel for me; 't is my picture;

210

	Refuse it not; it hath no tongue to vex you;
	And I beseech you come again tomorrow.
	What shall you ask of me that I'll deny,
	That honour saved may upon asking give?

VIOLA	Nothing but this: your true love for my master.

215

OLIVIA	How with mine honour may I give him that
	Which I have given to you?

VIOLA	I will acquit you.

OLIVIA	Well, come again tomorrow; fare you well;
	A fiend like thee might bear my soul to hell.

Exit.

Re-enter SIR TOBY BELCH and FABIAN.

SIR TOBY	Gentleman, God save thee.

220

VIOLA	And you, sir.

SIR TOBY	That defence thou hast, betake thee to 't; of what
	nature the wrongs are thou hast done him, I
	know not; but thy intercepter, full of despite,
	bloody as the hunter, attends thee at the orchard-

225

	end. Dismount thy tuck, be yare in thy
	preparation, for thy assailant is quick, skilful, and
	deadly.

VIOLA	You mistake, sir; I am sure no man hath any

3.4 Olivia's garden

Sir Toby makes Sir Andrew out to be a deadly swordsman, but promises to talk to him on Viola–Cesario's behalf.

230	**my remembrance ...** I have a very clear recollection.
233–234	**betake you to your guard ...** get ready to defend yourself.
235	**can furnish man withal** can equip a man with
237–238	He was knighted (**dubbed**) at court because he was good at being a courtier (**on carpet consideration**) and not in battle, where his sword (**rapier**) would have been hacked (**hatched**).
240–242	It is so impossible to calm his anger (**incensement**), that he will only be satisfied with your burial in a tomb (**sepulchre**).
242	**Hob, nob** 'Kill or be killed!'
244–245	**desire some conduct** ask for some protection
247–248	**taste their valour** to test how brave they are. Perhaps (**belike**) this is a man of that peculiar kind (**of that quirk**).
252–253	**unless you undertake ...** unless you're prepared to take me on, when you might just as safely fight with him
254–256	**for meddle you must ...** You'll have to fight or give up wearing a sword.
257–258	**I beseech you ...** I beg you, be so kind as to do this.
259–266	**something of my negligence ...** It is not something I've done intentionally.

| | quarrel to me; my remembrance is very free and clear from any image of offence done to any man. | 230 |

SIR TOBY   You'll find it otherwise, I assure you; therefore, if you hold your life at any price, betake you to your guard; for your opposite hath in him what youth, strength, skill, and wrath can furnish man withal.   235

VIOLA   I pray you, sir, what is he?

SIR TOBY   He is knight, dubbed with unhatched rapier, and on carpet consideration; but he is a devil in private brawl; souls and bodies hath he divorced three, and his incensement at this moment is so   240 implacable that satisfaction can be none but by pangs of death and sepulchre. Hob, nob, is his word; give 't or take 't.

VIOLA   I will return again into the house, and desire some conduct of the lady, I am no fighter. I have   245 heard of some kind of men that put quarrels purposely on others to taste their valour; belike this is a man of that quirk.

SIR TOBY   Sir, no; his indignation derives itself out of a very competent injury! Therefore get you on and give   250 him his desire. Back you shall not to the house, unless you undertake that with me which with as much safety you might answer him; therefore on, or strip your sword stark naked; for meddle you must, that's certain, or forswear to wear iron   255 about you.

VIOLA   This is as uncivil as strange. I beseech you, do me this courteous office, as to know of the knight what my offence to him is; it is something of my negligence, nothing of my purpose.   260

SIR TOBY   I will do so. Signior Fabian, stay you by this gentleman till my return.

Exit.

VIOLA   Pray you, sir, do you know of this matter?

3.4 Olivia's garden

Fabian tells Viola–Cesario how deadly Sir Andrew is, while, at the same time, Sir Toby is giving a similar picture of Viola–Cesario to Sir Andrew.

Activities

Actors' interpretations (18): the duel

Draw three or four frames of a storyboard, showing some of the highlights of the duel and the moments leading up to it (220–317). Then, in groups of four, try to 'block' the sequence (place actors in positions and work out moves). Act out the sequence and finally compare your version of the duel with other groups.

Viola (Imogen Stubbs) and Sir Andrew (Richard E Grant) in the 1996 film

264–266 **even to a mortal arbitrement** ... even so far as wanting a fight to the death, but I don't know anything more about it (**the circumstance more**)

268–270 He doesn't look (**to read him by his form**) as promising as you'll find him when you test out his bravery.

271 **bloody, and fatal opposite** bloodthirsty and deadly opponent

276 **had rather go with sir priest** ... I am peaceable by nature, rather than warlike.

279 **firago** female warrior

279 **I had a pass** I had a bout *(of fencing)*

280–283 He jabs his sword at me (**he gives me the stuck-in**) in such a deadly way (**with such a mortal motion**), that it is unavoidable; and, as you return his thrust (**on the answer**), he gets you.

284 **the Sophy** the Shah of Persia

285 **Pox on 't** a common oath

288–289 **an I thought** ... If I'd known he was so courageous and such a skilful fencer

293 **make the motion** tell him your offer

293–294 **make a good show on 't** try to look brave

294–295 **perdition of souls** loss of life

295–296 **ride** control and manipulate

| FABIAN | I know the knight is incensed against you, even to a mortal arbitrement, but nothing of the circumstance more. | 265 |

| VIOLA | I beseech you, what manner of man is he? | |

| FABIAN | Nothing of that wonderful promise, to read him by his form, as you are like to find him in the proof of his valour. He is indeed, sir, the most skilful, bloody, and fatal opposite that you could possibly have found in any part of Illyria. Will you walk towards him? I will make your peace with him if I can. | 270 |

| VIOLA | I shall be much bound to you for 't; I am one that had rather go with sir priest than sir knight; I care not who knows so much of my mettle. | 275 |

Exeunt.

Re-enter SIR TOBY with SIR ANDREW.

| SIR TOBY | Why, man, he's a very devil; I have not seen such a firago. I had a pass with him, rapier, scabbard, and all, and he gives me the stuck-in with such a mortal motion that it is inevitable; and on the answer, he pays you as surely as your feet hit the ground they step on. They say he has been fencer to the Sophy. | 280 |

| SIR ANDREW | Pox on 't, I'll not meddle with him. | 285 |

| SIR TOBY | Ay, but he will not now be pacified; Fabian can scarce hold him yonder. | |

| SIR ANDREW | Plague on 't; an I thought he had been valiant and so cunning in fence I'd have seen him damned ere I'd have challenged him. Let him let the matter slip, and I'll give him by horse, grey Capilet. | 290 |

| SIR TOBY | I'll make the motion. Stand here; make a good show on 't; this shall end without the perdition of souls. (*Aside*) Marry, I'll ride your horse as well as I ride you. | 295 |

3.4 Olivia's garden

Sir Toby, having been given Sir Andrew's horse to settle the quarrel, reassures Viola–Cesario that her opponent will not hurt her, but still desires a brief duel for the sake of his honour. Fabian says the same to Sir Andrew. As they reluctantly begin to fight, Antonio enters and, thinking that Sebastian is in danger, draws his sword to help him.

Activities

Character review: Antonio (3)

A Freeze-frame the moment at which Antonio enters and cries 'Put up your sword.'

B Think carefully about how each character should react at the moment of Antonio's entrance. Using the outline on page 210, sketch out your idea of the positions of each character on stage, and add thought-bubbles to show their unspoken reactions.

C Re-read the notes you made for the activity on page 108. Add further notes to explain how Shakespeare uses Antonio at this point in the play. Think about the way that:
- he provides a sudden serious contrast to the comedy
- he sets Viola thinking
- he permits later comic possibilities involving Sebastian
- he adds a dimension to the theme of 'love'. (What does his 'devotion' image in line 368 suggest about his feelings for Sebastian?)

297 **to take up the quarrel** to settle the argument

299 **He is as horribly conceited** ... he *(Cesario)* imagines him *(Andrew)* to be as terrifying

303 **for 's oath sake** so as not to go back on his word

303–304 **he hath better ...** he has thought better of his reasons for taking offence

306 **for the supportance of his vow** just so that he can keep his word

306 **he protests** he gives his assurance

308–309 It wouldn't take much (**A little thing**) to tell them (1) how great a coward I am; (2) that I am actually a woman (**how much I lack of a man**).

313 **by the duello** by the laws of duelling

320 **I for him defy you** I am challenging you on his behalf

321 **what are you?** What kind of person are you? What do you want?

3.4

Re-enter FABIAN and VIOLA.

(*To* FABIAN) I have his horse to take up the quarrel.
I have persuaded him the youth's a devil.

FABIAN   (*To* SIR TOBY) He is as horribly conceited of him;
and pants and looks pale, as if a bear were at his   300
heels.

SIR TOBY   (*To* VIOLA) There's no remedy, sir; he will fight
with you for 's oath sake. Marry, he hath better
bethought him of his quarrel, and he finds that
now scarce to be worth talking of; therefore draw   305
for the supportance of his vow; he protests he will
not hurt you.

VIOLA   (*Aside*)
Pray God defend me! A little thing would make
me tell them how much I lack of a man.

FABIAN   (*To* VIOLA) Give ground, if you see him furious.   310

SIR TOBY   Come, Sir Andrew, there's no remedy; the
gentleman will, for his honour's sake, have one
bout with you; he cannot by the duello avoid it;
but he has promised me, as he is a gentleman and
a soldier, he will not hurt you. Come on; to 't.   315

SIR ANDREW   Pray God, he keep his oath!

Draws his sword.

VIOLA   I do assure you, 't is against my will.

Draws her sword.

Enter ANTONIO.

ANTONIO   Put up your sword. If this young gentleman
Have done offence, I take the fault on me;
If you offend him, I for him defy you.   320

Drawing his sword.

SIR TOBY   You, sir! Why, what are you?

3.4 Olivia's garden

Angry at the interruption, Sir Toby is about to fight Antonio himself, when Orsino's officers arrive and arrest Antonio, who asks 'Sebastian' to return the money that he left with him earlier.

Activities

Shakespeare's language (14): changing meanings

In the four centuries since Shakespeare was writing, many words have changed their meanings – and others have gone completely out of use.

Can you remember what the following words mean today? You have met them all in the play so far. Discuss what you think the modern meanings are, and then look back through the notes to see how close you are.

i Words which have both their modern meaning and a different meaning in Shakespeare's language:

quick (1.1.9)	pains (2.2.5)
fancy (1.1.14)	politicians (2.3.72)
fell (1.1.21)	device (2.3.159)
cousin (1.3.5)	physic (2.3.163)
an (1.3.12)	complexion (2.4.26)
owe (2.4.104)	soft (2.5.94)

ii Words which are no longer used in modern standard English:

perchance (1.2.4)	betimes (2.3.2)
I prithee (1.2.50)	leman (2.3.26)
haply (1.2.52)	welkin (2.3.57)
quaffing (1.3.14)	maugre (3.1.155)
hither (2.2.3)	as lief (3.2.30)
fadge (2.2.32)	belike (3.3.25)

---

324 **undertaker** somebody who takes on another person's duties

328–330 **for that I promised you ...** *Andrew refers to the horse he promised, but, of course, Viola doesn't know what he's talking about.*

331 **thy office** your duty *(the officers are Orsino's police)*

332–333 **at the suit ...** on Orsino's instructions

334 **favour** appearance

337 **This comes with ...** This has happened because I have been looking for you.

339–340 **now my necessity Makes me** now that I need

340–342 **It grieves me ...** I am more upset that I can't help you, than because of what might happen to me.

342 **stand amazed** look bewildered

345 **entreat of you** ask you for

ANTONIO	One, sir, that for his love dares yet do more Than you have heard him brag to you he will.
SIR TOBY	Nay, if you be an undertaker, I am for you.

Draws.

FABIAN	O good Sir Toby, hold! Here come the officers.	325
SIR TOBY	I'll be with you anon.	
VIOLA	Pray, sir, put your sword up, if you please.	
SIR ANDREW	Marry, will I, sir; and, for that I promised you, I'll be as good as my word. He will bear you easily, and reins well.	330

Enter two OFFICERS.

FIRST OFFICER	This is the man; do thy office.	
SECOND OFFICER	Antonio, I arrest thee at the suit Of Count Orsino.	
ANTONIO	You do mistake me, sir.	
FIRST OFFICER	No, sir, no jot; I know your favour well, Through now you have no sea-cap on your head. Take him away; he knows I know him well.	335
ANTONIO	I must obey. (*To* VIOLA) This comes with seeking you; But there's no remedy; I shall answer it. What will you do, now my necessity Makes me to ask you for my purse? It grieves me Much more for what I cannot do for you Than what befalls myself. You stand amazed; But be of comfort.	340
SECOND OFFICER	Come, sir, away.	
ANTONIO	I must entreat of you some of that money.	345
VIOLA	What money, sir?	

Olivia's garden

Not recognising Antonio, Viola says that she knows nothing of any money but will lend him some of her own in gratitude for saving her. Antonio bitterly tells the officers how he is being denied by the youth he saved from drowning, and who had seemed virtuous.

Activities

Actor's interpretations (19): surprise

Freeze-frame the moment at which Antonio says 'you stand amazed' (342). Then, each character explains what she or he is thinking at that point.

Themes (7): appearance and reality

Discuss what Antonio's lines about Sebastian (370–375) say about appearance and reality.

Find other examples, from stories that you know, of beautiful looks covering up an ugly character. (The earliest might be the wicked Queen in *Snow White*.)

Character review: Viola (5)

'He named Sebastian . . .' Look back at Antonio's and Viola's words from Antonio's arrival to Viola's exit (318–390), and annotate the script to show where you think it gradually begins to dawn on Viola, and then to sink in, that her brother might still be alive.

349–352 Out of the small amount of money I have (**my lean and low ability**), I'll lend you something; I don't have much (**my having is not much**); I'll share with you (**make division of**) what I have at the present time (**my present**).

353–358 **Is 't possible that my deserts . . .** Can you really not be persuaded by what I deserve? Don't provoke me while I'm down (**tempt my misery**), or I might shame (**upbraid**) you by reminding you of all the generous things (**kindnesses**) I have done.

361–362 **any taint of vice . . .** any of the sin that we are born with

366 **Relieved him . . .** cared for him with religious devotion

367–370 **And to his image . . .** Antonio worshipped Sebastian, as though he were some holy statue. But (line 370) the 'god' proved to be a worthless idol.

371 **. . . done good feature shame** you have discredited good looks

372–375 **In nature . . .** The only real deformity in nature is in the minds of people who are unnatural and hard-hearted (**unkind**). Good people are beautiful; but evil people who look beautiful are like empty chests, decorated (**o'erflourished**) by the devil.

For the fair kindness you have showed me here,
And part, being prompted by your present trouble,
Out of my lean and low ability
I'll lend you something; my having is not much;   350
I'll make division of my present with you.
Hold, here is half my coffer.

ANTONIO   Will you deny me now?
Is 't possible that my deserts to you
Can lack persuasion? Do not tempt my misery,
Lest that it make me so unsound a man   355
As to upbraid you with those kindnesses
That I have done for you.

VIOLA   I know of none;
Nor know I you by voice or any feature.
I hate ingratitude more in a man
Than lying, vainness, babbling drunkenness,   360
Or any taint of vice whose strong corruption
Inhabits our frail blood.

ANTONIO   O heavens themselves!

SECOND   Come, sir, I pray you, go.
OFFICER

ANTONIO   Let me speak a little. This youth that you see here
I snatched one-half out of the jaws of death,   365
Relieved him with such sanctity of love,
And to his image, which methought did promise
Most venerable worth, did I devotion.

FIRST   What's that to us? The time goes by; away!
OFFICER

ANTONIO   But O! how vile an idol proves this god!   370
Thou hast, Sebastian, done good feature shame.
In nature there's no blemish but the mind;
None can be called deformed but the unkind;
Virtue is beauty, but the beauteous evil
Are empty trunks o'erflourished by the devil.   375

FIRST   The man grows mad; away with him! Come,
OFFICER   come, sir.

Olivia's garden

Hearing Antonio call her 'Sebastian', Viola begins to hope that her brother might be alive. Now realising that 'Cesario' is a coward, Sir Andrew goes off to beat him.

Activities

Character review: Viola (7)

Think about each of the following things that Viola has said. For each one, (a) try to remember when she said it and to whom (checking if necessary); and (b) say what you think it revealed about the kind of person she is:

- I will believe thou hast a mind that suit. With this thy fair and outward character
- Whoe'er I woo, myself would be his wife
- I swear I am not that I play
- I see you what you are; you are too proud
- As I am man, My state is desperate for my master's love
- She sat like Patience on a monument, Smiling at grief
- This fellow's wise enough to play the fool
- Then think you right; I am not what I am
- A little thing would make me tell them how much I lack of a man
- He named Sebastian.

379–382 Methinks his words ... Antonio has spoken with such passion, that he must believe what he has said. *Viola cannot bring herself to believe him; but she prays that her present dream will come true: that she has been mistaken for her brother, who must therefore be alive.*

384 a couplet or two ... one or two wise proverbs in verse

385–386 I my brother know ... *Because Sebastian is exactly like her, he comes to life every time she looks in the mirror.*

386–388 even such and so ... My brother looked just like this; and he always (**still**) went around dressed as I do now.

389 if it prove if this turns out to be true

393 denying him refusing to recognise or acknowledge him

395 devout ... *Fabian imagines Cesario's cowardice to be so much part of his make-up that it is a religion to him.*

396 'Slid By God's eyelid!

398 An I do not 'If I don't beat him, never trust me!'

400 I dare lay any money ... I'm willing to bet any money that it won't come to anything!

ANTONIO	Lead me on.

Exeunt OFFICERS with ANTONIO.

VIOLA	Methinks his words do from such passion fly,	
	That he believes himself; so do not I.	380
	Prove true, imagination, O! prove true,	
	That I, dear brother, be now ta'en for you.	

SIR TOBY	Come hither, knight; come hither, Fabian; we'll
	whisper o'er a couplet or two of most sage saws.

VIOLA	He named Sebastian; I my brother know	385
	Yet living in my glass; even such and so	
	In favour was my brother; and he went	
	Still in this fashion, colour, ornament,	
	For him I imitate. O! if it prove,	
	Tempests are kind, and salt waves fresh in love.	390

Exit.

SIR TOBY	A very dishonest paltry boy, and more a coward
	than a hare. His dishonesty appears in leaving his
	friend here in necessity, and denying him; and for
	his cowardship, ask Fabian.

FABIAN	A coward, a most devout coward, religious in it.	395

SIR ANDREW	'Slid, I'll after him again, and beat him.

SIR TOBY	Do; cuff him soundly, but never draw thy sword.

SIR ANDREW	An I do not, –

Exit.

FABIAN	Come, let's see the event.

SIR TOBY	I dare lay any money 't will be nothing yet.	400

Exeunt.

Exam practice

Plot review (4): Characters and strands

In pairs, draft a chart with annotations to show how each character is connected to each of the three plot-strands: (a) the love-triangle; (b) the aftermath of the shipwreck; and (c) the revenge against Malvolio.
Predict how the three strands of the plot will unfold:

1. What can happen to ease the lovers' difficulties?
2. How can Viola and Sebastian be united?
3. Who will be the ultimate victor in the war between Malvolio and the household?

Actors' interpretations (20)

A In pairs look back through 3.4 and discuss (i) exactly what Malvolio says and does to make Olivia think he is mad; (ii) what Sir Toby and Fabian say and do in order to frighten Viola–Cesario and Sir Andrew before they fight their duel.

B 1. The sequence in which Malvolio appears to Olivia in yellow stockings and is then taunted by Sir Toby and the others (3.4.17–127) can be extremely funny on stage. Explain in detail how you think Shakespeare provides opportunities for comedy in this scene. Before you begin to write you should think about:
   - the comedy which comes from Malvolio's appearance
   - the things Malvolio says to Olivia
   - Olivia's reactions
   - the way Malvolio follows the instructions and advice of the letter
   - his reactions to Sir Toby and the others when they treat him as though he were mad.

   2. The sequence in which the terrified Viola and equally terrified Sir Andrew are brought together to fight their duel (3.4.220–317) can be extremely funny on stage. Explain in detail how you think Shakespeare provides opportunities for comedy in this scene. Before you begin to write you should think about:
   - the language that Sir Toby and Fabian use to make the two duellists frightened
   - the ways in which Viola's and Sir Andrew's terror can be shown on stage
   - Viola's asides
   - the way Sir Toby cheats Sir Andrew out of his horse.

C Using 3.4 as a particular example, write a short essay on the nature of the comedy in *Twelfth Night*. Concentrate particularly on the way in which the dialogue and the actors' appearance and movements combine to create the comic effects.

Shakespeare's language (15): imagery

A In 1.5 to get across the idea that love dominates his thoughts, Orsino describes it as being like the sea, swallowing everything up. What would you compare love to? In pairs, think up five lines to help explain the ideas that:
- love is wonderful when it starts, but always becomes disappointing and miserable
- love is always complicated
- love is the best thing imaginable
- love is painful
- love can take you over.

B In 1.5 Orsino uses many images to explain what he thinks love is and to describe his feelings for Olivia. For example:
- 1–3: Music is the food that love feeds on.
- 10–11: Love is all-consuming like the sea.
- 20–22: Orsino is 'hounded' by his desires, like a hart pursued by fierce dogs.

- 28–31: Olivia will weep salt water to keep the love for her brother fresh (like preserving food).
- 34–36: When Olivia loves Orsino, Cupid's arrow will kill 'the flock' of all the other loves within her.
- 36–38: All her 'thrones' (liver, brain and heart – the sources of love) will be filled with one king.

1. Pick one or more of these images and draw a cartoon or a picture which represents what you see in your mind's eye.
2. Create three images yourself (words, rather than drawings), which help to explain a feature of love, hate, anger, or some other strong emotion. Try to mimic Orsino's own poetic style.
3. Create a poster (either a collage or your own drawing) to illustrate Antonio's feelings about his love for Sebastian in 3.4 366–370.

C Write about the way in which the imagery in 1.5 and 3.4 contributes to the theme of love and reveals much about Orsino's and Antonio's characters. What range of references do the characters use (Orsino begins with food), in attempting to convey their ideas about love? How effective are the images in expressing the different aspects of love? What does the imagery reveal about the characters?

4.1 A street outside Olivia's house

Sebastian is mistaken for Viola–Cesario, first by Feste who has been sent by Olivia, and then by Sir Andrew, who strikes him.

<table>
<tr><td>

Activities

Themes (8): appearance and reality

Thinking that he is talking to Cesario, Feste says, 'No, I do not know you . . . Nothing that is so is so.'

Re-read the other two activities on the theme of appearance and reality and write down your impressions of how important this theme seems to be to the play as a whole.

</td></tr>
</table>

1   **Will you make me believe** Are you trying to tell me

5   **Well held out, i' faith!** You're keeping up the pretence (of pretending I don't know you) very well.

10–11   **vent thy folly . . .** Play your stupid games somewhere else; you do not know me.

12   **Vent my folly!** *Feste mocks Sebastian's language (also in lines 16 and 17): he is used to Cesario speaking more like a servant.*

14–15   **I am afraid this great lubber . . .** I'm afraid this great lumbering fool, the world, will now start using affected language.

15–16   **I prithee now . . .** *Feste uses pompous language himself, mocking Sebastian, to tell him to give up (**ungird**) his odd behaviour (in pretending not to know him).*

18   **foolish Greek** stupid joker *(from 'merry Greek', a common expression)*

20   **worse payment** *Presumably he will hit him.*

21   **By my troth . . .** Truly, you are very generous! *(Cesario has already given him money. See 3.1.44.)*

23   **report** reputation

23   **after fourteen years' purchase** after they've paid more than it's worth

Act 4

Scene 1

The street before Olivia's house.

Enter SEBASTIAN and FESTE.

FESTE   Will you make me believe that I am not sent for
           you?

SEBASTIAN Go to, go to; thou art a foolish fellow;
           Let me be clear of thee.

FESTE   Well held out, i' faith! No, I do not know you;   5
           nor I am not sent to you by my lady to bid you
           come speak with her; nor your name is not
           Master Cesario; nor this is not my nose neither.
           Nothing that is so is so.

SEBASTIAN I prithee, vent thy folly somewhere else;   10
           Thou know'st not me.

FESTE   Vent my folly! He has heard that word of some
           great man, and now applies it to a fool. Vent my
           folly! I am afraid this great lubber, the world, will
           prove a cockney. I prithee now, ungird thy   15
           strangeness and tell me what I shall vent to my
           lady. Shall I vent to her that thou art coming?

SEBASTIAN I prithee, foolish Greek, depart from me;
           There's money for thee; if you tarry longer
           I shall give worse payment.   20

FESTE   By my troth, thou hast an open hand. These wise
           men that give fools money get themselves a good
           report – after fourteen years' purchase.

Enter SIR ANDREW.

SIR ANDREW Now, sir, have I met you again? There's for you.

Striking SEBASTIAN.

SEBASTIAN Why, there's for thee, and there, and there.   25

Beating SIR ANDREW.

4.1 A street outside Olivia's house

Sir Toby tries to restrain Sebastian from beating Sir Andrew. As swords are drawn, Olivia enters and orders Sir Toby to leave her sight.

Activities

Character review: Sebastian (2)

Having left Antonio for a few hours, to look around the sites of Illyria, Sebastian suddenly undergoes a series of extremely baffling experiences.

(A) List the odd things which happen to Sebastian after his arrival.

(B) Imagine you are working for Illyria Radio and are producing some programmes on tourism in your country. Next week's programme is called Impressions of a Tourist. Improvise an interview with Sebastian, and get his comments on the encounters with a strange fool, a blond assailant with a heavily built accomplice, and a beautiful – and extremely seductive – countess!

(C) Write an article for the *Illyria Times* (which could be based on material gained from the interview in B, above, or on your own preparation), headed A Visitor to Illyria. Include direct quotes from Sebastian, as he recounts the bizarre things that have happened to him since his arrival. In particular, try to reflect the sense that there is a kind of 'madness' around.

28–29 **in some of your coats** *Compare the modern expression 'in your shoes'.*

31–33 **I'll go another way to work ...** I'll find another way to deal with him: I'll charge him with assault (**have an action of battery against him**).

33–34 **Though I struck him first ...** *Which, of course, is why Andrew could not charge Sebastian!*

36–37 **my young soldier** *Toby thinks he is talking to Cesario, mocking him for his cowardice.*

37 **put up your iron** put your sword away

37 **well fleshed** you've had a taste of blood

39 **What would'st thou now?** What do you want now?

42 **malapert** impudent

45 **Will it be ever thus?** Is it always going to be like this?

45 **Ungracious** uncivilised

47 **preached** taught

48 **dear Cesario** *Olivia uses the name 'Cesario', as Feste did, so that the audience see clearly that a major misunderstanding is about to take place.*

49 **Rudesby** ruffian

Are all the people mad?

Enter SIR TOBY and FABIAN.

SIR TOBY   Hold, sir, or I'll throw your dagger o'er the house.

They seize SEBASTIAN.

FESTE   This will I tell my lady straight. I would not be in
some of your coats for twopence.

SIR TOBY   Come on, sir; hold.   30

SIR ANDREW   Nay, let him alone; I'll go another way to work
with him; I'll have an action of battery against
him if there be any law in Illyria. Though I struck
him first, yet it's no matter for that.

SEBASTIAN   Let go thy hand.   35

SIR TOBY   Come, sir, I will not let you go. Come, my young
soldier, put up your iron; you are well fleshed,
come on.

SEBASTIAN   I will be free from thee. What would'st thou now?
If thou dar'st tempt me further, draw thy sword.   40

SIR TOBY   What, what! Nay, then I must have an ounce or
two of this malapert blood from you.

Draws his sword.

Enter OLIVIA.

OLIVIA   Hold, Toby! On thy life I charge thee, hold!

SIR TOBY   Madam!

OLIVIA   Will it be ever thus? Ungracious wretch!   45
Fit for the mountains and the barbarous caves,
Where manners ne'er were preached. Out of my
  sight!
Be not offended, dear Cesario.
(*To SIR TOBY*) Rudesby, be gone!

Exeunt SIR TOBY, SIR ANDREW and FABIAN.

4.2 Olivia's house

Mistaking him for 'Cesario' Olivia invites Sebastian to go back to the house with her. Thinking that he must be dreaming, he willingly agrees. As Scene 2 begins, Feste is disguising himself as Sir Topas, the curate.

Activities

Character review: Malvolio (5)

In order to revise what you know about Malvolio before encountering him again, think about each of the following things that he has said. For each one, (a) try to remember when he said it and to whom (checking if necessary); and (b) say what you think it revealed about the kind of person he is:

- I marvel your ladyship takes delight in such a barren rascal
- He is very well-favoured, and he speaks very shrewishly
- if it be worth stooping for, there it lies in your eye
- My masters, are you mad, or what are you?
- she shall know of it, by this hand
- I extend my hand to him thus
- I thank my stars I am happy
- Sweet lady, ho, ho
- 'Be not afraid of greatness'; 't was well writ
- You are idle, shallow things; I am not of your element.

50–52 **Let thy fair wisdom ...** Be ruled by your intelligence, rather than your emotions in this barbarous and lawless (**uncivil and unjust**) attack (**extent**) on your peace.

54–55 **that thou thereby ...** so that, hearing of Toby's other stupidities, you will be able to laugh at this one

56 **Beshrew his soul** Curse him!

57 **He started ...** He made my poor heart jump with fear.

58 **What relish ...?** What's going on here?

59 **Or ... or** either ... or

60 **Let fancy still ...** May love (**fancy**) for ever (**still**) keep my senses plunged in the river of forgetfulness (**Lethe**).

2 **Sir** *a title used by priests at that time.* **Topas** *(or topaze) is a precious stone once used to cure lunatics.*

4 **dissemble myself** (1) disguise myself; (2) behave like a hypocrite

7 **to become the function well** to perform the role properly

8–10 **but to be said ...** but to be called respectable (**honest**) and hospitable (**a good housekeeper**) is as good as being called hard-working (**careful**) and a great scholar

11 **competitors** fellow-plotters, partners in the joke

>   I prithee, gentle friend,
> Let thy fair wisdom, not thy passion, sway   50
> In this uncivil and unjust extent
> Against thy peace. Go with me to my house,
> And hear thou there how many fruitless pranks
> This ruffian hath botched up, that thou thereby
> May'st smile at this. Thou shalt not choose but go;   55
> Do not deny. Beshrew his soul for me,
> He started one poor heart of mine in thee.

SEBASTIAN What relish is in this? How runs the stream?
Or I am mad, or else this is a dream.
Let fancy still my sense in Lethe steep;   60
If it be thus to dream, still let me sleep!

OLIVIA Nay; come, I prithee; would thou 'dst be ruled by
me!

SEBASTIAN Madam, I will.

OLIVIA   O! say so, and so be.

Exeunt.

Scene 2

A room in Olivia's house.

Enter MARIA and FESTE.

MARIA Nay, I prithee, put on this gown and this beard,
make him believe thou art Sir Topas the curate;
do it quickly; I'll call Sir Toby the whilst.

Exit.

FESTE Well, I'll put it on, and I will dissemble myself in
't; and I would I were the first that ever   5
dissembled in such a gown. I am not tall enough
to become the function well, nor lean enough to
be thought a good student; but to be said an
honest man and a good housekeeper goes as
fairly as to say a careful man and a great scholar.   10
The competitors enter.

4.2 Olivia's house

Pretending to be Sir Topas, Feste torments Malvolio in his darkened prison, treating him as though he were mad and claiming that the room is well lit.

Activities

Character review: Feste (4)

An actor will often prepare for a play by asking 'what are my aims in each scene?' As you work through 4.2, write down the ways in which Feste fulfils each of the following aims:

- to impersonate 'Sir Topas'
- to treat Malvolio as though he were mad by pretending that (i) he is possessed by the devil; (ii) the room is not dark; (iii) his opinions are those of a madman.

Can you think of any other aims that Feste might have in this scene? If so, state what they are and note how Feste fulfils them.

---

13 ***Bonos dies*** *incorrect Latin for 'Good day'*

13–17 **the old hermit ...** *Feste has made up this character to sound like a scholar who utters wise sayings such as 'That that is is' and he follows them up with mock logic.*

19 **Peace in this prison** *Priests usually said 'Peace in this house' when visiting the sick.*

20 **knave** lad

20 **counterfeits** acts the part

26 **hyperbolical fiend** greatest of devils

26–27 **How vexest thou ...** How you torment this man!

32 **Fie** *a common exclamation to show that you disagreed strongly – something like 'Rubbish!'*

32 **thou dishonest Satan** you lying devil

32–33 **most modest** gentlest

37–38 **transparent as barricadoes** as see-through as barricades. *Similes usually work by comparing like with like (e.g. 'as white as snow'); Feste deliberately makes them nonsense (like his reference to the* **south-north***).*

38 **clerestories** high windows *which usually let in a lot of light*

39 **lustrous** shining; **ebony** is a black wood

Act 4 Scene 2

Enter SIR TOBY BELCH and MARIA.

SIR TOBY	Jove bless thee, Master Parson.
FESTE	*Bonos dies*, Sir Toby; for, as the old hermit of Prague, that never saw pen and ink, very wittily said to a niece of king Gorboduc, "That that is is"; so I, being Master Parson, am Master Parson, for what is "that" but "that", and "is" but "is"?

15

SIR TOBY	To him, Sir Topas.
FESTE	(*Calling*) What ho! I say. Peace in this prison.
SIR TOBY	The knave counterfeits well; a good knave.

20

MALVOLIO	(*Calling from within*) Who calls there?
FESTE	Sir Topas the curate, who comes to visit Malvolio the lunatic.
MALVOLIO	Sir Topas, Sir Topas, good Sir Topas, go to my lady.

25

FESTE	Out, hyperbolical fiend! How vexest thou this man! Talkest thou nothing but of ladies?
SIR TOBY	Well said, Master Parson.
MALVOLIO	Sir Topas, never was man thus wronged. Good Sir Topas, do not think I am mad; they have laid me here in hideous darkness.

30

FESTE	Fie, thou dishonest Satan! I call thee by the most modest terms; for I am one of those gentle ones that will use the devil himself with courtesy. Sayest thou that house is dark?

35

MALVOLIO	As hell, Sir Topas.
FESTE	Why, it hath bay windows transparent as barricadoes, and the clerestories toward the south-north are as lustrous as ebony; and yet complainest thou of obstruction?

40

4.2 Olivia's house

Feste continues to torment Malvolio by asking questions about the soul as a supposed test of his sanity, but Sir Toby feels that it is not safe to carry the trickery any further.

Activities

Character review: Sir Toby (2)

In the drama of seeing Malvolio taunted by Feste, it is easy to miss a very interesting speech by Sir Toby. Re-read lines 69–74 and discuss the following questions:

1. What mood should Sir Toby be in here (triumphant, anxious, despondent . . .)?
2. Why might he be 'so far in offence' with Olivia that he doesn't consider it safe to carry the trick against Malvolio any further?
3. What is he worried Olivia might do?
4. To whom is he saying 'Come by and by to my chamber' – Feste or Maria? Discuss what the line might mean, depending upon who is being addressed.

---

43 **thou errest** (1) you are mistaken; (2) you are a sinner

44 **puzzled** lost in ignorance

45 *One of the plagues inflicted upon the Egyptians in the Bible was a thick fog.*

49–50 **make the trial of it . . .** Check my sanity by testing my powers of reasoning.

51–52 **Pythagoras** *was an ancient Greek philosopher who taught that, when a person died, their soul entered an animal.*

56 **think nobly . . .** *Malvolio holds the Christian belief that souls are immortal.*

56–57 **no way approve . . .** I do not agree at all with his opinion.

58 **darkness** (1) absence of light in the room; (2) ignorance or sin

59–60 **ere I will allow of thy wits** before I will agree that you are sane

60–61 **lest thou dispossess . . .** for fear that you might leave your grandmother without a home

64 **exquisite** brilliant

65 **I am for all waters** I can have a go at anything.

69–73 **I would we were well rid of this knavery . . .** *Toby has offended Olivia so much that he cannot continue the trick on Malvolio without risking further trouble.*

70–71 **conveniently delivered** released without too much fuss

MALVOLIO	I am not mad, Sir Topas. I say to you, this house is dark.
FESTE	Madman, thou errest; I say there is no darkness but ignorance, in which thou art more puzzled than the Egyptians in their fog. 45
MALVOLIO	I say this house is as dark as ignorance, though ignorance were as dark as hell; and I say there was never man thus abused. I am no more mad than you are; make the trial of it in any constant question. 50
FESTE	What is the opinion of Pythagoras concerning wild fowl?
MALVOLIO	That the soul of our grandam might haply inhabit a bird.
FESTE	What thinkest thou of his opinion? 55
MALVOLIO	I think nobly of the soul, and no way approve his opinion.
FESTE	Fare thee well; remain thou still in darkness. Thou shalt hold the opinion of Pythagoras ere I will allow of thy wits, and fear to kill a woodcock, lest 60 thou dispossess the soul of thy grandam. Fare thee well.
MALVOLIO	Sir Topas! Sir Topas!
SIR TOBY	My most exquisite Sir Topas!
FESTE	(*To* SIR TOBY) Nay, I am for all waters. 65
MARIA	Thou might'st have done this without thy beard and gown; he sees thee not.
SIR TOBY	To him in thine own voice, and bring me word how thou findest him. (*To* MARIA) I would we were well rid of this knavery. If he may be conveniently 70 delivered, I would he were; for I am now so far in offence with my niece that I cannot pursue with

4.2 Olivia's house

Hearing Feste singing his own voice, Malvolio calls out and begs him to fetch pen and paper so that he can write to Olivia.

Activities

Character review: Feste (5)

A Give examples of the things that Feste says to Malvolio, in order to treat him as though he were actually mad.

B 1. Discuss how Feste deals with: (a) Malvolio's comment that the prison is dark; (b) Malvolio's response to the question about Pythagoras (51–61). What do you think of Feste's behaviour with Malvolio here? Is it funny, in your opinion, or vicious and nasty?

2. Act out the scene, up to line 62, performing it in two different ways: (a) where you try to bring out the humour and are generally on Feste's side; (b) where you show sympathy for a Malvolio being badly treated by a sadistic Feste.

Then discuss which version seems in tune with your overall interpretation of the play.

(Continued on page 152)

73–74 Come by and by ... Come to my bedroom in a minute.

78 *perdy* by God

83 as ever thou wilt deserve ... if you want to be richly rewarded by me

89 how fell you ...? How did you come to lose your senses?

90 notoriously abused shamefully ill-treated. *(Notoriously is used three more times in the play to describe his treatment. Abused appeared earlier (line 48) and is later used by Olivia.)*

92 But ... Only as well as me (*a fool?*)

94 propertied me treated me as though I were an object without feelings

96 to face me out of my wits to deceive me into thinking I am mad

97 Advise you be careful

98–99 thy wits the heavens restore may heaven restore your sanity

99 Endeavour ... try to sleep

100 vain bibble-babble meaningless prattle

any safety this sport to the upshot. Come by and
by to my chamber.

Exeunt SIR TOBY and MARIA.

FESTE (*Singing*)
         Hey Robin, jolly Robin,   75
         Tell me how thy lady does.

MALVOLIO   Fool!

FESTE   *My lady is unkind, perdy*

MALVOLIO   Fool!

FESTE   *Alas! why is she so?*   80

MALVOLIO   Fool, I say!

FESTE   *She loves another.* Who calls, ha?

MALVOLIO   Good fool, as ever thou wilt deserve well at my
hand, help me to a candle, and pen, ink, and
paper. As I am a gentleman, I will live to be   85
thankful to thee for 't.

FESTE   Master Malvolio!

MALVOLIO   Ay, good fool.

FESTE   Alas, sir, how fell you besides your five wits?

MALVOLIO   Fool, there was never man so notoriously abused;   90
I am as well in my wits, fool, as thou art.

FESTE   But as well? Then you are mad indeed, if you be
no better in your wits than a fool.

MALVOLIO   They have here propertied me; keep me in
darkness, send ministers to me, asses! and do all   95
they can to face me out of my wits.

FESTE   Advise you what you say; the minister is here. (*As
SIR TOPAS*) Malvolio, Malvolio, thy wits the
heavens restore! Endeavour thyself to sleep, and
leave thy vain bibble-babble.   100

4.2 Olivia's house

After pretending that Sir Topas has returned, Feste at last agrees to help Malvolio and he goes off singing.

Activities

C If you were directing this scene, what might you suggest to the actor playing Feste about his motivation here? There are a number of unanswered questions, open to interpretation. What exactly is he doing to Malvolio here, and why is he doing it? How far is he acting on Sir Toby's or Maria's instructions and how far is this his own embellishment to the plot? Why does he decide finally that he will bring Malvolio the writing materials he needs?

Actor's interpretations (21): Feste and Malvolio

4.3 calls for some skilful acting. Among other things, the actor playing Feste has to:

• imitate 'Sir Topas'
• argue cleverly (37–62)
• switch voices (75–105)

While the actor playing Malvolio has to:
• sound desperate
• be unwillingly polite to Feste (83–123)

In pairs, act out the scene, paying attention to the acting points listed.

102 **Maintain no words ...** do not speak with him

107 **I am shent** I have been told off

112 **Well-a-day ...** Oh, I only wish you were, sir!

115–116 **it shall advantage thee ...** You will get more out of this than you ever got before from carrying a letter.

117–121 **are you not mad indeed ...** You are mad really, aren't you? Or are you faking it? *Feste continues to punish Malvolio, by suggesting that he still appears to be genuinely mad. He goes on to demand proof that Malvolio has any brains at all (...* **till I see his brains***).*

122 **requite** reward you

128–135 ***the old Vice** a wicked character from medieval morality plays. In Feste's song, he is imagined as carrying a dagger made of a strip of wood (***lath***), with which he would cut (***Pare***) the devil's (his dad's) nails.*

MALVOLIO   Sir Topas!

FESTE   Maintain no words with him, good fellow. (*As
            FESTE*) Who, I, sir? Not I, sir. God be wi' you, good
            Sir Topas. (*As SIR TOPAS*) Marry, amen ... (*As FESTE*)
            I will, sir, I will.   105

MALVOLIO   Fool, fool, fool, I say!

FESTE   Alas, sir, be patient. What say you, sir? I am shent
            for speaking to you.

MALVOLIO   Good fool, help me to some light and some
            paper; I tell thee I am as well in my wits as any   110
            man in Illyria.

FESTE   Well-a-day, that you were, sir!

MALVOLIO   By this hand, I am. Good fool, some ink, paper,
            and light; and convey what I will set down to my
            lady; it shall advantage thee more than ever the   115
            bearing of letter did.

FESTE   I will help you to 't. But tell me true, are you not
            mad indeed, or do you but counterfeit?

MALVOLIO   Believe me, I am not; I tell thee true.

FESTE   Nay, I'll ne'er believe a madman till I see his   120
            brains. I will fetch you light and paper and ink.

MALVOLIO   Fool, I'll requite it in the highest degree; I prithee,
            be gone.

FESTE (*Singing*)
                            I am gone, sir,
                            And anon, sir,   125
                        I'll be with you again,
                            In a trice
                        Like to the old Vice,
                        Your need to sustain;

                        Who with dagger of lath,   130
                        In his rage and his wrath,
                            Cries, Ah, ha! to the devil;

4.3 Olivia's garden

Sebastian seems to have walked into a dream and has to convince himself that neither he nor Olivia is mad. He misses Antonio's advice and wonders what has happend to him.

Activities

Actors' interpretations (22): Scenes

In the 1969 production, it was possible to hear Malvolio from his prison even after Sebastian had entered. Donald Sinden describes the moment like this: 'with a scream I fall to the bottom of the pit. Silence. Daylight comes. Sebastian enters: (lines 1–4:) "... Yet, 't is not madness." A very weak cry of "Help!" comes from below ground, unheard by Sebastian ... (4–10:) "That this may be some error but no madness ..." An almost incoherent sentence containing the word "help" is heard.
(10–15:) Sebastian talks on: "... To any other trust but that I am mad ..." A faint sound of nonsensical gibberish can be heard trailing off into sobs.'

Perform the sequence as Sinden describes it and discuss what effects can be achieved if it is done in this way.

135   ***goodman*** good master

6–7   **Yet there he was** Yet he had been there, and I gained this information (**credit**), that he was going around (**did range**) the town trying to find me.

8   **counsel** advice

9–13   **For though my soul disputes ...** For, even though all my feelings are in agreement with my senses, that this might be a mistake, but isn't madness, this great good fortune which has come my way (**accident and flood ...**) is so much more amazing than anything that has happened before (**So far exceed all instance ...**), that I am willing to disbelieve my senses.

14–16   **And wrangle with my reason ...** *This forces him to argue against the reasoning, and conclude that the only credible solution is that he or Olivia must be mad.*

17   **sway her house** govern the household

18   **Take and give back affairs ...** undertake business and see it through

19   **stable bearing** controlled manner

20–21   **... deceivable** There's something not at all right here.

26   **Plight me the full assurance ...** assure me fully of your good faith by promising to marry me

4.3

> *Like a mad lad,*
> *Pare thy nails, dad;*
> *Adieu, goodman devil.* 135

Exit.

Scene 3

Olivia's garden.

Enter SEBASTIAN.

SEBASTIAN   This is the air; that is the glorious sun;
This pearl she gave me, I do feel 't and see 't;
And though 't is wonder that enwraps me thus,
Yet 't is not madness. Where's Antonio then?
I could not find him at the Elephant; 5
Yet there he was, and there I found this credit,
That he did range the town to seek me out.
His counsel now might do me golden service;
For though my soul disputes well with my sense
That this may be some error, but no madness, 10
Yet doth this accident and flood of fortune
So far exceed all instance, all discourse,
That I am ready to distrust mine eyes,
And wrangle with my reason that persuades me
To any other trust but that I am mad 15
Or else the lady's mad; yet if 't were so,
She could not sway her house, command her
    followers,
Take and give back affairs and their dispatch
With such a smooth, discreet, and stable bearing
As I perceive she does. There's something in 't 20
That is deceivable. But here the lady comes.

Enter OLIVIA and a PRIEST.

OLIVIA   Blame not this haste of mine. If you mean well,
Now go with me and with this holy man
Into the chantry by; there, before him,
And underneath that consecrated roof, 25
Plight me the full assurance of your faith,
That my most jealous and too doubtful soul
May live at peace. He shall conceal it

4.3 Olivia's garden

To Olivia's great joy, Sebastian agrees to marry her and they follow the priest to the chapel.

Activities

Themes (9): madness

Re-read Sebastian's speech and make notes on what it adds to the theme of madness in the play. For example, what evidence is leading Sebastian to believe that he must be mad? How does he reassure himself that Olivia is not mad? Look back at the other two activities on the theme of madness and write down your impressions of how important this theme seems to be to the play as a whole.

---

29 **Whiles . . .** until you are ready for it to be made public

30 **What time** and then, at that time

31 **According to my birth** *The wedding would fit her rank of countess.*

35 **fairly note** bless

	Whiles you are willing it shall come to note,	
	What time we will our celebration keep	30
	According to my birth. What do you say?	
SEBASTIAN	I'll follow this good man, and go with you;	
	And, having sworn truth, ever will be true.	
OLIVIA	Then lead the way, good father; and heavens so shine	
	That they may fairly note this act of mine!	35

Exeunt.

Exam practice

Character review: Malvolio (6)

Donald Sinden (Malvolio in 1969) said: 'Shakespeare in no way prepares his audience for the shock of Malvolio's next appearance.' When we see him in this scene, he is locked up in some kind of darkened prison, and is often portrayed as physically exhausted, filthy and desperate to be released. In the 1969 production, Malvolio had been placed in 'some type of primitive septic tank covered firstly by an iron grille and over that a trap door to keep out some of the disgusting smell'. In 1997, Philip Voss's Malvolio was placed in a dog kennel with a collar around his neck and 'with all the filth and degradation that goes with it'.

A Re-read 3.4.137–144, to recap on what it is exactly that Sir Toby and the others had planned to do to Malvolio, in order to keep up his punishment after he had appeared to Olivia in yellow stockings. Where were they going to put him? How were they going to punish him? What opinion did they want other people to have of him?

B In many productions we are encouraged to feel sorry for Malvolio in this scene, as we see him unhappy and bewildered in his prison. Bearing that in mind:

1. Discuss how you would stage the scene. How would you represent the 'dark room'? What do you think of the dog kennel idea, for example?
2. What state would you have Malvolio in? Dirty, with torn clothes? Or simply a slightly untidy version of his normal self?

Either draw an annotated sketch, or write a brief account, to describe what you think the setting for 4.2 should look like, and how you think Malvolio should appear.

C   Discuss how much sympathy an audience should be feeling for Malvolio in this scene, in your opinion (bearing in mind that this should fit your interpretation of Malvolio in the play as a whole). One way of engendering a lot of sympathy is by making his prison conditions appalling and representing him as desperately unhappy and confused. On the other hand, the scene can be played in a spirit of light-hearted comedy in which the sympathy is still substantially with the revengers.

Plot review (5): The three strands

There is only one scene of the play remaining. Discuss how far the complications in each of the three plot-strands (the love-triangle; the revenge on Malvolio; and the aftermath of the shipwreck) have been resolved, and which major problems remain to be sorted out. For example, the problem of Olivia's love for Cesario seems to have been partly solved by her marriage to Sebastian. But what difficulties does that solution itself create? The problems include:

(a) in the love-triangle:
- Orsino's continuing love for Olivia
- Viola's secret love for Orsino (who thinks she is a boy)

(b) in the revenge:
- Malvolio's wrongful imprisonment (a problem for him, and also for the others when the truth becomes known)

(c) in the aftermath of the shipwreck:
- Antonio's arrest and bitterness at being let down by Sebastian
- the twins' continued loss of each other.

Character review: Maria (2)

The script does not give Maria another appearance after her exit in 4.2.

A   Discuss in pairs how far Maria's plot against Malvolio has worked. What did she originally plan to do? What, in fact, has happened? (First look back at 2.3.)

B   Compose the entries that (i) Maria and (ii) Sir Toby might write in their diaries after leaving Feste with Malvolio (4.2.74). What would each of them say about:
- the plot against Malvolio and how far it has succeeded;
- future problems (for example, when Olivia finds out what has happened);
- their relationship with each other (look back, for example, at 2.3.175–176; at the activity on p. 148; and ahead to 5.1.359–361).

Try to show the different perspectives that each one would have on both the revenge against Malvolio and their relationship with each other.

C   Write about your impressions of the relationship between Sir Toby and Maria. What does the script reveal, and what opportunities does the script provide for interesting interpretations when the play is performed. (You may wish to refer to particular productions, such as the Trevor Nunn film with Mel Smith as Sir Toby and Imelda Staunton as Maria.) It will help to look ahead to 5.1.359–361.

5.1 A street near Olivia's house

Feste refuses to let Fabian see the letter that Malvolio has written to Olivia and then, when Orsino arrives, entertains him with some witty wordplay.

Activities

Character review: Feste (5)

A When 5.1 begins, Feste is taking Malvolio's letter to Olivia. Imagine you are Feste. Write down and explain your thoughts and feelings about what has happened to Malvolio and your part in the trickery. You could begin: From my point of view, it all goes back a long way . . .

Before you begin to write you should decide what Feste thought and felt about:

- Malvolio's position in the household
- Malvolio's Puritanism (see page 211)
- Malvolio's attitude towards him, his role in the household and his jokes
- Malvolio's humiliation of him in front of Olivia in Act 1
- Malvolio's words and behaviour in 2.3.

(Continued on page 162)

1 **as thou lovest me** a common expression, implying 'Please . . . I am your friend!'

1 **his** Malvolio's

5–6 *Queen Elizabeth once asked a courtier to grant her what she wanted and promised in return to grant a request of his. He agreed, and she asked for his pet dog, which he gave her. His request in return was that she would give the dog back!*

7–8 **Belong . . .** *The word implies that they are objects, an idea Feste mocks with* **trappings** *(ornaments).*

12 **Just the contrary** Surely you mean the opposite?

18 **abused** treated badly *(by being deceived)*

19 **conclusions to be as kisses** *This refers to a poem in which a girl refused to be kissed, saying 'No!' twice. Feste's speech is all about 'double negatives' see the activity on this page.*

Act 5

Scene 1

The street before Olivia's house.

Enter FESTE and FABIAN.

FABIAN	Now, as thou lovest me, let me see his letter.
FESTE	Good Master Fabian, grant me another request.
FABIAN	Any thing.
FESTE	Do not desire to see this letter.
FABIAN	This is, to give a dog, and in recompense desire 5 my dog again.

Enter DUKE, VIOLA, CURIO and attendants.

DUKE	Belong you to the Lady Olivia, friends?
FESTE	Ay, sir; we are some of her trappings.
DUKE	I know thee well; how dost thou, my good fellow?
FESTE	Truly, sir, the better for my foes and the worse for 10 my friends.
DUKE	Just the contrary; the better for thy friends.
FESTE	No, sir, the worse.
DUKE	How can that be?
FESTE	Marry, sir, they praise me and make an ass of me; 15 now my foes tell me plainly I am an ass; so that by my foes, sir, I profit in the knowledge of myself, and by my friends I am abused; so that, conclusions to be as kisses, if your four negatives make your two affirmatives, why then, the worse 20 for my friends and better for my foes.
DUKE	Why, this is excellent.
FESTE	By my troth, sir, no; though it please you to be one of my friends.

5.1 A street near Olivia's house

After begging more money from Orsino, Feste goes to fetch Olivia. When Antonio is brought in, Orsino recognises him as a former enemy.

Activities

B 1. Discuss how far you agree with the following descriptions of Feste (all from Stephen Boxer, who played him in 1997):

(a) 'He is inconsistent ... quite gifted ... anarchic [lawless] ... enigmatic [puzzling].'

(b) 'He'll do almost anything for money.'

(c) 'If the situation's too hot, he'll shoot off – he won't burn his own fingers.'

(d) 'His raison d'être [reason for living] is to make people laugh.'

(e) 'Like a juggler, he's keeping the balls in the air.'

(f) 'He's very intuitive [acts by instinct].'

2. What do you make of Feste's 'This will I tell my lady straight ...'? Which of Stephen Boxer's statements seems to refer to it?

C Using the statements from Stephen Boxer (in B above) as a basis, make notes for an essay on Feste which will discuss the idea that he is an outsider with no real friendship for other characters, except for a close attachment to Olivia.

26–27 **double-dealing** cheating *(with a wordplay on the idea of doubling what he has received)*

28 **ill counsel** bad advice

30 **obey it** obey my bad advice *(to double the money)*

33 ***Primo . . .*** 'First-second-third' is a good children's game (**play**).

34 **the third pays for all** third time lucky

34–35 ***triplex . . .*** the triple-time is a good skipping rhythm

41–45 *Feste will sing a lullaby to Orsino's generosity (**bounty**) until it has finished its nap.*

42–44 I wouldn't want you to think that my desire to have your money is the sin of greed (**covetousness**).

48–49 **besmeared As black as Vulcan** *The Roman god was always covered in soot from working at his forge, making armour.*

50 **baubling** small and insignificant

51 not worth capturing as a prize (**unprizable**) because it was very lightweight (of **shallow draught** – not deep underwater)

52–55 He engaged in such a harmful fight (**scathful grapple**) with the best of our ships (**the most noble bottom of our fleet**), that even those who had reason to hate him, because they lost by the battle (**very envy and the tongue of loss**), admired him (**Cried fame and honour . . .**).

5.1

| DUKE | Thou shalt not be the worse for me; there's gold. | 25 |

Gives him money.

| FESTE | But that it would be double-dealing, sir, I would you could make it another. |

| DUKE | O! you give me ill counsel. |

| FESTE | Put your grace in your pocket, sir, for this once, and let your flesh and blood obey it. | 30 |

| DUKE | (*Giving him more money*) Well, I will be so much a sinner to be a double-dealer; there's another. |

| FESTE | *Primo, secundo, tertio,* is a good play; and the old saying is, the third pays for all; the *triplex,* sir, is a good tripping measure; or the bells of Saint Bennet, sir, may put you in mind: one, two, three. | 35 |

| DUKE | You can fool no more money out of me at this throw; if you will let your lady know I am here to speak with her, and bring her along with you, it may awake my bounty further. | 40 |

| FESTE | Marry, sir, lullaby to your bounty till I come again. I go, sir; but I would not have you to think that my desire of having is the sin of covetousness; but as you say, sir, let your bounty take a nap; I will awake it anon. | 45 |

Exit.

| VIOLA | Here comes the man, sir, that did rescue me. |

Enter ANTONIO and OFFICERS.

| DUKE | That face of his I do remember well; Yet, when I saw it last, it was besmeared As black as Vulcan in the smoke of war. A baubling vessel was he captain of, For shallow draught and bulk unprizable; With which such scathful grapple did he make With the most noble bottom of our fleet, That very envy and the tongue of loss Cried fame and honour on him. What's the matter? | 50 ... 55 |

5.1 A street near Olivia's house

Viola identifies Antonio as the man who took her side in the duel. Antonio tells Orsino how he had rescued the 'ungrateful boy' and lent him money which he refused to give back.

Activities

Character review: Antonio (4)

1. Hot-seat Antonio, asking him:
   - what he expects will happen to him, now that he has been arrested
   - what feelings he had for Sebastian when he left him earlier
   - what he thinks of Sebastian now
   - how he accounts for Orsino's puzzling assertion that 'this youth' has been in his service for three months.

2. Read this explanation of Antonio's speech (82–88) and then improvise it, trying to bring out his bitterness:
   Where being apprehended ... And, when I was arrested, his clever deceitfulness (**false cunning**) – since he didn't want to share (**partake**) my danger – enabled him to pretend that he didn't know me (**to face me out of his acquaintance**); and, within a second (**While one would wink**), he behaved as though we hadn't met for twenty years, and refused to give me (**denied me**) my own purse, which, only half an hour earlier, I had allowed him (**recommended**) to use.

---

57 **took the Phoenix and ...** captured the *Phoenix* and her cargo from Crete

60 **desperate of shame ...** caring nothing about what people thought of him, or the position he was in

61 We arrested (**did we apprehend**) him in the middle of a private argument (**brabble**).

63 But, having done so (**in conclusion**), he spoke to me very strangely (**put strange speech upon me**).

64 **I know not ...** I can only assume it was a fit of madness.

65 **Notable** notorious

66–68 **What foolish boldness ...?** What kind of stupid courage put you at the mercy of people who had become your enemies in such a bloody and costly way (**in terms so bloody and so dear**)?

69 **Be pleased that ...** Please allow me to

71 **on base and ground enough** with very good reason

75 **redeem** save

77–78 **without retention ...** given freely, dedicated to him

79 **pure** only

80 **adverse** hostile

81 **beset** attacked

90 **for three months** *This also lets us know how much time Viola has been with Orsino.*

FIRST OFFICER	Orsino, this is that Antonio That took the Phoenix and her fraught from Candy; And this is he that did the Tiger board, When your young nephew Titus lost his leg. Here in the streets, desperate of shame and state, 60 In private brabble did we apprehend him.
VIOLA	He did me kindness, sir, drew on my side; But in conclusion put strange speech upon me; I know not what 't was but distraction.
DUKE	Notable pirate! thou salt-water thief! 65 What foolish boldness brought thee to their mercies, Whom thou, in terms so bloody and so dear, Hast made thine enemies?
ANTONIO	Orsino, noble sir, Be pleased that I shake off these names you give me; Antonio never yet was thief or pirate, 70 Though I confess, on base and ground enough, Orsino's enemy. A witchcraft drew me hither; That most ungrateful boy there by your side, From the rude sea's enraged and foamy mouth Did I redeem; a wreck past hope he was; 75 His life I gave him, and did thereto add My love, without retention or restraint, All his in dedication; for his sake Did I expose myself, pure for his love, Into the danger of this adverse town; 80 Drew to defend him when he was beset; Where being apprehended, his false cunning, Not meaning to partake with me in danger, Taught him to face me out of his acquaintance, And grew a twenty-years-removèd thing 85 While one would wink, denied me mine own purse, Which I had recommended to his use Not half an hour before.
VIOLA	How can this be?
DUKE	When came he to this town?
ANTONIO	Today, my lord, and for three months before, 90

5.1 A street near Olivia's house

When Olivia enters she refuses to listen to Orsino's words of love. Suspecting that Olivia loves 'Cesario', Orsino threatens to kill 'him'.

91   **No interim ...** without a single break or interval

95   **tended upon me** been my servant

97–98   **What would my lord, but ...** What do you want, apart from what you cannot have (my love).

104–106   **If it be aught ...** If it is anything to do with the usual 'tune' *(Orsino's offer of marriage)*, it is as boring and distasteful (**fat and fulsome**) to my ear as a dog howling.

108   **perverseness** deliberate refusal to do the sensible thing

108   **uncivil** rude, discourteous

109–111   *Seeing her as some kind of goddess (line 93:* **Now heaven walks on earth**), *Orsino claims that his soul has made the most faithful sacrifices* (**offerings hath breathed**) *on her ungrateful and unlucky* (**ingrate and unauspicious**) *altar, that any devoted person has ever offered up.*

112   **Even what it please ...** Do whatever you think is fitting.

114–115   *An Egyptian thief in a popular story tried to kill his lover, rather than let her be captured.*

116   **savours nobly** has touches of nobility in it

5.1

No interim, not a minute's vacancy,
Both day and night did we keep company.

Enter OLIVIA and attendants.

DUKE	Here comes the countess; now heaven walks on earth!
	(*To* ANTONIO) But for thee, fellow; fellow, thy words are madness;
	Three months this youth hath tended upon me; 95
	But more of that anon. (*To the* OFFICERS) Take him aside.
OLIVIA	What would my lord, but that he may not have,
	Wherein Olivia may seem serviceable?
	Cesario, you do not keep promise with me.
VIOLA	Madam! 100
DUKE	Gracious Olivia, –
OLIVIA	What do you say, Cesario? Good my lord, –

Signs to prevent ORSINO from speaking.

VIOLA	My lord would speak; my duty hushes me.
OLIVIA	If it be aught to the old tune, my lord,
	It is as fat and fulsome to mine ear, 105
	As howling after music.
DUKE	Still so cruel?
OLIVIA	Still so constant, lord.
DUKE	What, to perverseness? You uncivil lady,
	To whose ingrate and unauspicious altars
	My soul the faithfull'st offerings hath breathed out 110
	That e'er devotion tendered! What shall I do?
OLIVIA	Even what it please my lord, that shall become him.
DUKE	Why should I not, had I the heart to do it,
	Like to the Egyptian thief at point of death,
	Kill what I love? A savage jealousy 115
	That sometimes savours nobly. But hear me this:

5.1 A street near Olivia's house

When Viola–Cesario prepares to follow Orsino dutifully, Olivia feels betrayed. Viola–Cesario denies being Olivia's husband.

Activities

Actors' interpretations (23): a dramatic moment

The moment when Olivia says 'Cesario, husband, stay' (139) can be very powerful on stage, as all the characters react to it in different ways.

A Freeze-frame the moment, working hard to bring out each character's reactions.

B Using the stage outline on page 210, draw a sketch of the scene, perhaps based on a freeze-frame, and add thought-bubbles to show what each character is thinking after Olivia has uttered the word 'husband'.

C Write notes on the challenges and opportunities facing anyone directing this moment in the play. Think about features such as blocking (actors' positions and movements), and how best to convey characters' emotions and reactions.

117–120 **Since you to non-regardance ...** Since you reject my love, and since I have a good idea of (**partly know**) the person who forces me out of the true place in your affections (**favour**), live on as a hard-hearted tyrant.

121 **minion** darling

122 **tender** care for

125 **ripe in mischief** ready to do something terrible

128 **jocund, apt** happy and ready

129 **To do you rest** to give you peace of mind

132 **More, by all mores ...** more than anything you can compare it with

133 **witnesses above** the gods

134 **tainting of** being unfaithful to

135 **Ah me, detested ...!** He hates me! I have been deceived!

137 **forgot thyself?** forgotten who you are (my husband)?

142–143 **Alas! it is the baseness ...** Oh, it is your miserable cowardice which is making you suppress your real identity (**strangle thy propriety**) as my husband.

144–146 **take thy fortunes up ...** accept your new position in life: behave like the person you know you really are, and then you will be as great as the person you fear (Orsino)

	Since you to non-regardance cast my faith,	
	And that I partly know the instrument	
	That screws me from my true place in your favour,	
	Live you the marble-breasted tyrant still;	120
	But this your minion, whom I know you love,	
	And whom, by heaven I swear, I tender dearly,	
	Him will I tear out of that cruel eye,	
	Where he sits crownéd in his master's spite.	
	(*To* VIOLA) Come, boy, with me; my thoughts are ripe	
	in mischief;	125
	I'll sacrifice the lamb that I do love,	
	To spite a raven's heart within a dove.	

VIOLA

And I, most jocund, apt, and willingly,
To do you rest, a thousand deaths would die.

OLIVIA

Where goes Cesario?

VIOLA

                    After him I love   130
More than I love these eyes, more than my life,
More, by all mores, then e'er I shall love wife.
If I do feign, you witnesses above,
Punish my life for tainting of my love!

OLIVIA

Ah me, detested! how am I beguiled!   135

VIOLA

Who does beguile you? Who does do you wrong?

OLIVIA

Hast thou forgot thyself? Is it so long?
Call forth the holy father.

DUKE

(*To* VIOLA)   Come, away!

OLIVIA

Whither, my lord? Cesario, husband, stay.

DUKE

Husband!

OLIVIA

               Ay, husband; can he that deny?   140

DUKE

Her husband, sirrah!

VIOLA

                  No, my lord, not I.

OLIVIA

Alas! it is the baseness of thy fear
That makes thee strangle thy propriety.
Fear not, Cesario; take thy fortunes up;

5.1 A street near Olivia's house

The priest confirms that Olivia and 'this youth' have just got married. As Orsino expresses his bitterness, Sir Andrew enters with a head-wound.

Activities

Shakespeare's language (18): oaths and interjections

Sir Andrew's 'For the love of God' is one of the many oaths and interjections used by characters throughout the play.

Look at the following examples and try to remember (a) which character used the expression; and (b) (where it isn't obvious) what it means: What a plague (1.3.1); Fie (1.3.25); By this hand (1.3.34); Marry (1.3.66); Faith (1.3.100); Alas the day (2.1.24); By 'r lady (2.3.61); Beshrew me (2.3.77); 'Slight (2.5.34) ; Pox on 't. (3.4.285); Plague on 't (3.4.288); 'Slid (3.4.396).

Actors' interpretations (24): Dramatic moments

Look back at the activity on 'Cesario, husband . . .' (page 168). Then write an essay on 'The Staging of *Twelfth Night*', focusing on moments which offer particularly exciting opportunities for actors and directors. You might consider Malvolio's interruption of the revellers in 2.3; Malvolio reading the letter; his appearance in yellow stockings; the duel and Antonio's interruption; and Olivia calling 'Cesario, husband . . .' (5.1.139). A further moment of this kind is to come with Malvolio's entrance in line 323.

147–148 **I charge thee . . .** I order you, on your word as a priest (**by your reverence**), to tell these people (**Here to unfold**)

149–150 **To keep in darkness . . .** to keep secret what the present circumstances (**occasion**) have made public earlier than intended (**before 't is ripe**)

153–154 **Confirmed by mutual joinder . . .** confirmed by joining of hands, demonstrated (**attested**) by a holy kiss

157 **Sealed in my function, by my testimony** confirmed through my role as priest and witness

160 **dissembling cub!** deceitful foxcub! *(the fox is associated with cunning; 'cub' because Cesario is still young)*

161 **sowed a grizzle . . .** sprinkled grey hairs on your coat (**case**) – 'by the time you have a grey beard'

162–163 **Or will not else . . .** Or maybe your cunning (**craft**) will grow so quickly that it will trip you up and be your downfall.

167 **Hold little faith . . .** Trust me a little, despite your fear.

169 **presently** immediately

171 **broke my head across** smashed me over the head

172 **bloody coxcomb** bleeding head *('cock's comb')*

Be that thou know'st thou art, and then thou art   145
As great as that thou fear'st.

Enter PRIEST.

                            O welcome, father!
Father, I charge thee, by thy reverence,
Here to unfold, though lately we intended
To keep in darkness what occasion now
Reveals before 't is ripe, what thou dost know   150
Hath newly passed between this youth and me.

PRIEST   A contract of eternal bond of love,
Confirmed by mutual joinder of your hands,
Attested by the holy close of lips,
Strengthened by interchangement of your rings;   155
And all the ceremony of this compact
Sealed in my function, by my testimony;
Since when, my watch hath told me, toward my
     grave
I have travelled but two hours.

DUKE   O thou dissembling cub! what wilt thou be   160
When time hath sowed a grizzle on thy case?
Or will not else thy craft so quickly grow
That thine own trip shall be thine overthrow?
Farewell, and take her; but direct thy feet
Where thou and I henceforth may never meet.   165

VIOLA   My lord, I do protest, –

OLIVIA   O! do not swear;
Hold little faith, though thou hast too much fear.

Enter SIR ANDREW AGUECHEEK.

SIR ANDREW   For the love of God, a surgeon! Send one
presently to Sir Toby.

OLIVIA   What's the matter?   170

SIR ANDREW   He has broke my head across, and has given Sir
Toby a bloody coxcomb too. For the love of God,
your help! I had rather than forty pound I were at
home.

5.1 A street near Olivia's house

Sir Andrew claims that he has been attacked by 'Cesario'. Sir Toby enters, drunk and also wounded. When Sir Andrew offers to help, Sir Toby rejects him.

Activities

Shakespeare's language (19): malapropisms

Sir Andrew calls Sebastian 'the very devil incarnadine' (177). He means 'incarnate' (in a body, rather than a spirit), but perhaps gets mixed up with 'cardinal'. A mistake of this kind has come to be known as a malapropism, after a character called Mrs Malaprop in Sheridan's *The Rivals*, written in 1775. Do some research on the speech of the following, to see how malapropisms are used for humour:

- Bottom in *A Midsummer Night's Dream*
- Mistress Quickly in *Henry V*
- Dogberry in *Much Ado About Nothing*.

Actors' interpretations (25): Sir Andrew and Sir Toby

Rehearse and act out lines 168–203. First discuss how far you would wish to emphasise:

- Sir Toby's drunkenness
- his injuries
- his cruelty to Sir Andrew
- Sir Andrew's injuries
- his reaction to Cesario
- his friendship for Sir Toby
- his hurt at being rejected by Sir Toby.

Think carefully about how each character should exit.

179	**'Od's lifelings!** By God's little life!
180–181	**And that that I did . . .** Sir Toby made me do whatever I did!
184	**bespake you fair** spoke politely to you
186	**I think you set nothing by . . .** I don't believe you think a bleeding head is important!
187	**halting** limping
188	**in drink** drunk
189	**tickled you other-gates . . .** dealt with you differently (giving you more than a tickle with his sword)
192	**Sot** (1) fool; (2) drunkard
193–194	**an hour agone . . .** He's been drunk for the past hour. In fact, he was unconscious (**his eyes were set**) at eight o'clock this morning.
195	**passy-measures pavin** *Sir Toby is possibly likening the drunken doctor's walk to a kind of slow dance.*
197	**havoc** mess
199	**dressed** bandaged up
201–202	**ass-head . . . coxcomb . . . gull** *All words for 'fool'. Gull has the special meaning of someone who can be easily fooled (as in gullible).*
203	**let his hurt . . .** someone take care of his wound

OLIVIA	Who has done this, Sir Andrew?	175

SIR ANDREW The count's gentlemen, one Cesario; we took him
for a coward, but he's the very devil incardinate.

DUKE My gentleman, Cesario?

SIR ANDREW 'Od's lifelings! here he is. (*To* VIOLA) You broke my
head for nothing! And that that I did, I was set on   180
to do 't by Sir Toby.

VIOLA Why do you speak to me? I never hurt you;
You drew your sword upon me without cause;
But I bespake you fair, and hurt you not.

SIR ANDREW If a bloody coxcomb be a hurt, you *have* hurt me;   185
I think you set nothing by a bloody coxcomb.

Enter SIR TOBY BELCH and FESTE.

Here comes Sir Toby halting; you shall hear more;
but if he had not been in drink he would have
tickled you other-gates than he did.

DUKE How now, gentlemen! how is 't with you?   190

SIR TOBY That's all one; has hurt me, and there's the end on
't. (*To* FESTE) Sot, didst see Dick surgeon, sot?

FESTE O! he's drunk, Sir Toby, an hour agone; his eyes
were set at eight i' the morning.

SIR TOBY Then he's a rogue, and a passy-measures pavin. I   195
hate a drunken rogue.

OLIVIA Away with him! Who hath made this havoc with
them?

SIR ANDREW I'll help you, Sir Toby, because we'll be dressed
together.   200

SIR TOBY Will you help? An ass-head, and a coxcomb, and
a knave, a thin-faced knave, a gull!

OLIVIA Get him to bed, and let his hurt be looked to.

Exeunt FESTE, FABIAN, SIR TOBY and SIR ANDREW.

5.1 A street near Olivia's house

When Sebastian enters to apologise for injuring Sir Toby, everyone looks at him and Viola in amazement. Then the twins see each other but can hardly believe that they have been reunited.

Activities

Actors' interpretations (26): 'One face ... and two persons.'

1. Using the plan on page 210, sketch out a stage plan to show how you think the characters ought to be positioned at the moment of Sebastian's entrance (204).
   First think about:
   - which characters have to be able to see both Sebastian and Viola
   - how many of the characters Sebastian can be allowed to see
   - which characters have to speak first.

2. Then block the scene (actually place actors in their positions) from lines 204 to 221 and decide upon movements which would help to reveal the characters' changing reactions, including the moments when:
   - Olivia initially reacts on seeing Sebastian and Cesario together
   - Orsino comments on the twins' appearance (211–212)
   - Sebastian suddenly spots Antonio (213–215)
   - Antonio responds (216–219)
   - Olivia expresses further amazement (220)
   - Sebastian notices Viola (221).

---

206 **with wit and safety** in order to protect myself

207–208 **You throw a strange regard ...** You are looking at me strangely, and I can tell (**do perceive**) that my behaviour has upset you.

211 **habit** set of clothes

212 **A natural perspective ...** *Orsino refers to a special glass which can create two images, when there is actually only one object.*

216 **Fear'st thou that ...?** Are you questioning that?

218 **cleft** sliced

222–223 **Nor can there be that deity ...** and nature cannot have that god-like ability to be everywhere at once

224 **devoured** swallowed up

225 **Of charity ...** out of kindness

229 **So went he suited ...** This was how he was dressed when he drowned.

230 **If spirits ...** if evil spirits can take on the shape and clothing of the living

232–233 **But am in that ...** but my soul is contained in the same bodily form (**dimension**) that I have had since my birth (**from the womb**)

234 **as the rest goes even** as you appear to be from everything else (except your clothing)

Enter SEBASTIAN.

SEBASTIAN	I am sorry, madam, I have hurt your kinsman;
	But had it been the brother of my blood, 205
	I must have done no less with wit and safety.
	You throw a strange regard upon me, and by that
	I do perceive it hath offended you;
	Pardon me, sweet one, even for the vows
	We made each other but so late ago. 210
DUKE	One face, one voice, one habit, and two persons;
	A natural perspective, that is, and is not!
SEBASTIAN	Antonio! O my dear Antonio!
	How have the hours racked and tortured me
	Since I have lost thee! 215
ANTONIO	Sebastian are you?
SEBASTIAN	Fear'st thou that, Antonio?
ANTONIO	How have you made division of yourself?
	An apple cleft in two is not more twin
	Than these two creatures. Which is Sebastian?
OLIVIA	Most wonderful! 220
SEBASTIAN	(*Noticing* VIOLA) Do I stand there? I never had a
	brother;
	Nor can there be that deity in my nature,
	Of here and every where. I had a sister,
	Whom the blind waves and surges have devoured.
	(*To* VIOLA) Of charity, what kin are you to me? 225
	What countryman, what name, what parentage?
VIOLA	Of Messaline; Sebastian was my father;
	Such a Sebastian was my brother too,
	So went he suited to his watery tomb.
	If spirits can assume both form and suit 230
	You come to fright us.
SEBASTIAN	A spirit I am indeed;
	But am in that dimension grossly clad
	Which from the womb I did participate.
	Were you a woman, as the rest goes even,

A street near Olivia's house

Viola and Sebastian confirm their identity. As Sebastian explains Olivia's error to her, Orsino realises that Viola loves him.

Activities

Character review: Viola (7)

A Look back through Act 5 and make notes on how you think Viola's feelings might change as the scene progresses. What might she be feeling:
- when Antonio is brought in (46)
- when Olivia speaks to her (99)
- when Orsino calls her to his side (125)
- when Olivia calls her 'husband' (139)
- when the priest confirms their marriage (152–159)
- when Sir Andrew accuses her of beating him up (176)
- when Sebastian enters (204)
- when Orsino proposes marriage (321–322)?

B Basing your ideas on the references in A, above, write director's notes to guide the actress playing Viola, on what emotions she might be undergoing throughout this scene.

C Her qualities. Discuss which of Viola's qualities are apparent from her behaviour in Act 5. In particular, consider the opportunities that an actress has to show that Viola is an active heroine, who is able to take matters into her own hands, rather than one who is merely passively reacting to the behaviour and actions of others.

241 **that record ...** I can remember that so clearly.

242 **mortal act** life

244 **If nothing lets ...** if there is nothing else preventing us from being happy, except for the man's clothes which I have taken over (**masculine usurped attire**)

247 **do cohere and jump** fit exactly together and agree

250 **weeds** clothes

252 **All the occurrence ...** everything that has since happened to me

255 **But nature to her bias drew ...** Nature followed its usual tendency to bring together the male and the female *(just as, in bowls, the wood rolls in a curve, according to the 'bias', or weighted side)*.

256 **contracted** promised in marriage

257–258 **Nor are you therein ...** and you are not mistaken in that: you are engaged both to a man and a 'maid' *(maid could mean a male virgin)*

260 **glass** The perspective glass's illusion *(see line 212)* is still turning out to be real.

264 **over-swear** swear all over again

266–267 **As doth that orbéd continent the fire ...** *Viola will remain as true as the sun.*

I should my tears let fall upon your cheek,   235
And say "Thrice welcome, drownéd Viola!"

VIOLA   My father had a mole upon his brow.

SEBASTIAN   And so had mine.

VIOLA   And died that day when Viola from her birth
              Had numbered thirteen years.   240

SEBASTIAN   O! that record is lively in my soul.
              He finishéd indeed his mortal act
              That day that made my sister thirteen years.

VIOLA   If nothing lets to make us happy both,
              But this my masculine usurped attire,   245
              Do not embrace me till each circumstance
              Of place, time, fortune, do cohere and jump
              That I am Viola; which to confirm,
              I'll bring you to a captain in this town,
              Where lie my maiden weeds; by whose gentle help 250
              I was preserved to serve this noble count.
              All the occurrence of my fortune since
              Hath been between this lady and this lord.

SEBASTIAN   (*To* OLIVIA) So comes it, lady, you have been
                  mistook,
              But nature to her bias drew in that.   255
              You would have been contracted to a maid;
              Nor are you therein, by my life, deceived.
              You are betrothed both to a maid and man.

DUKE   Be not amazed; right noble is his blood.
              If this be so, as yet the glass seems true, 260
              I shall have share in this most happy wreck.
              (*To* VIOLA) Boy, thou hast said to me a thousand
                  times
              Thou never should'st love woman like to me.

VIOLA   And all those sayings will I over-swear,
              And all those swearings keep as true in soul 265
              As doth that orbéd continent the fire
              That severs day from night.

5.1 A street near Olivia's house

Viola remembers that Malvolio has had the Sea Captain arrested and Feste reports on Malvolio's 'madness'. When Feste is told to read Malvolio's letter he does so in a madman's voice.

Activities

Character review: Orsino (6)

1. How believable is Orsino's sudden offer of marriage to Viola (whom he has thought of as a boy called Cesario for three months!)? Discuss:
   - the reasons which seem to make it unbelievable
   - the exact words Orsino uses to propose marriage (are they very romantic?)
   - the things that might be done throughout the play to prepare the audience for Orsino's apparently sudden change of heart (think about what might happen in his scenes with Cesario earlier in the play, and the way in which his 'love' for Olivia can be presented).

2. Discuss Helen Schlesinger's view that 'In a way Viola and Orsino are seeing each other for the first time. It's scary. An unrequited [not returned] love is in a way quite an easy thing to live with.'

270–271 **he upon some action . . .** He is being held in custody (**in durance**) because of some lawsuit by Malvolio *(who seems to have accused him of something)*.

273 **enlarge** release

275 **much distract** mad

276–277 **A most extracting frenzy . . .** A madness which forced everything else out of my mind, made me totally forget his madness.

278 **sirrah** *a term of address to servants*

279–280 **he holds Belzebub . . .** He keeps the devil at a distance (**at the stave's end**), as well as anybody in his circumstances (**case**) can do.

282–284 **as a madman's epistles . . .** Since a madman's letters aren't 'the gospel truth', it doesn't much matter (**skills not**) when they are delivered.

286–287 **Look then to be well edified . . .** Prepare to be well informed, when a fool reports (**delivers**) a madman's message.

290–292 **an your ladyship . . .** If you want it to be realistic, I have to use the right voice.

294 **his right wits** in his (Malvolio's) actual state of mind – madness

295 **perpend** listen carefully

DUKE	Give me thy hand;
	And let me see thee in thy woman's weeds.

VIOLA	The captain that did bring me first on shore
	Hath my maid's garments; he upon some action 270
	Is now in durance at Malvolio's suit,
	A gentleman, and follower of my lady's.

OLIVIA	He shall enlarge him. Fetch Malvolio hither.
	And yet, alas, now I remember me,
	They say, poor gentleman, he is much distract. 275
	A most extracting frenzy of mine own
	From my remembrance clearly banished his.

Re-enter FESTE, with a letter, and FABIAN.

(*To FESTE*) How does he, sirrah?

FESTE	Truly, madam, he holds Belzebub at the stave's
	end as well as a man in his case may do. Has here 280
	writ a letter to you; I should have given it you
	today morning; but as a madman's epistles are no
	gospels, so it skills not much when they are
	delivered.

OLIVIA	Open 't, and read it. 285

FESTE	Look then to be well edified when the fool
	delivers the madman.
	(*Reads*) *By the Lord, madam,* –

OLIVIA	How now! art *thou* mad?

FESTE	No, madam, I do but read madness; an your 290
	ladyship will have it as it ought to be, you must
	allow *vox*.

OLIVIA	Prithee, read i' thy right wits.

FESTE	So I do, madonna; but to read his right wits is to
	read thus; therefore perpend, my princess, and 295
	give ear.

OLIVIA	(*To FABIAN*) Read it *you*, sirrah.

5.1 A street near Olivia's house

Olivia tells Fabian to read the letter out, and then instructs him to bring Malvolio to her. Orsino proposes to Viola and Malvolio arrives.

Activities

Actors' interpretations (27): Malvolio's letter

Feste's reading of Malvolio's letter in a madman's voice can be very funny. Discuss, however, how an audience might also be made to feel that the message in the letter is rather sad.

1. Improvise a scene in Malvolio's prison as he reads the letter over to himself, before giving it to Feste to deliver. Think carefully about how much sympathy you want the audience to have for him.

2. Then act out lines 286–310, making Feste's reading as 'mad' as possible.

3. Finally give Fabian's reading. But first discuss what view of the situation Fabian has at this point. Is he:
   - worried that he might get into trouble?
   - determined to impress Olivia by seeming to be the only sensible servant left?
   - embarrassed about reading a personal letter out loud?
   - regretting the whole thing because Malvolio has been punished too severely?
   - and is he a good reader? (Robert Lindsay's Fabian in the BBC version actually stumbled over some of the words.)

302–303 ***induced me to the semblance*** ... persuaded me to dress and behave as I did

304 ***do myself much right*** ... I am sure that the letter will prove me right, or cause you to feel ashamed.

305–306 It is the wrong done to me (***my injury***) which is making me forget to speak respectfully (***leave my duty a little unthought of***).

310 **This savours not** ... This doesn't sound much like madness.

311 **delivered** released

312–313 **these things further thought on** ... When you have had time to consider all this, please be as happy that I am your sister-in-law, as you would have been had I been your wife.

314 **crown the alliance** formally celebrate our relationship (of brother- and sister-in-law)

315 **at my proper cost** at my own expense

316 **most apt** very ready to accept (**embrace**) your offer

317 **quits you** releases you from his service

318 **mettle of your sex** your natural feminine behaviour

322 **A sister! You are she** *Olivia is Viola's sister-in-law by her marriage to Sebastian.*

FABIAN (*Reading*)
> *By the Lord, madam, you wrong me, and the world*
> *shall know it; though you have put me into darkness,*
> *and given your drunken cousin rule over me, yet have*   300
> *I the benefit of my senses as well as your ladyship. I*
> *have your own letter that induced me to the*
> *semblance I put on; with the which I doubt not but to*
> *do myself much right, or you much shame. Think of*
> *me as you please. I leave my duty a little unthought of,*   305
> *and speak out of my injury.*

> THE MADLY-USED MALVOLIO

OLIVIA   Did he write this?

FESTE   Ay, madam.

DUKE   This savours not much of distraction.   310

OLIVIA   See him delivered, Fabian; bring him hither.

> *Exit FABIAN.*

My lord, so please you, these things further thought
    on,
To think me as well a sister as a wife,
One day shall crown the alliance on 't, so please
    you,
Here at my house and at my proper cost.   315

DUKE   Madam, I am most apt to embrace your offer.
(*To* VIOLA) Your master quits you; and for your
    service done him,
So much against the mettle of your sex,
So far beneath your soft and tender breeding,
And since you called me master for so long,   320
Here is my hand; you shall from this time be
Your master's mistress.

OLIVIA   A sister! You are she.

> *Re-enter FABIAN, with MALVOLIO.*

DUKE   Is this the madman?

5.1 A street near Olivia's house

Malvolio asks Olivia to account for his treatment. When she sees the letter she explains to Malvolio that he has been tricked. Fabian tells her how it happened and who was responsible.

Activities

Actors' interpretations (28): Malvolio's entrance

A Freeze-frame the moment, discussing first how each character should react.

B Malvolio breaks dramatically into the atmosphere of celebration. Rehearse a scene in which Olivia says: 'A sister! You are she', celebratory music breaks out, and Malvolio enters in the middle of people congratulating each other and laughing . . . The music fades away, silence falls and Orsino speaks . . .

C Discuss where Malvolio should appear from (off stage? a prison on-stage? what kind of prison?) and how he should look when he enters (dignified? dirty and dishevelled? humiliated?) – (a) if you want the audience to sympathise with him; and (b) if you want the audience simply to laugh at him.

Helena Bonham-Carter (Olivia) and Nigel Hawthorne (Malvolio)

328 **You must not now . . .** You cannot possibly deny

329 **Write from it** write differently

330 **your invention** something you have written yourself

332 **in the modesty of honour** in the name of decent behaviour

333 **lights** signs

336 **lighter** inferior

340 **geck and gull** foolish, gullible person

341 **That e'er invention . . .** who was ever the subject of a practical joke

343 **character** style of handwriting

347–348 **in such forms . . .** in the appearance which was suggested to you beforehand (**presupposed Upon thee**) in the letter

349 **This practice . . .** This joke has been played (**passed**) upon you very cleverly and cruelly (**most shrewdly**).

350 **the grounds and authors** the reasons for it and those responsible

351–352 **plaintiff** *Malvolio will bring the case and judge it.*

354 **Taint the condition . . .** spoil the present atmosphere

358–359 **Upon some stubborn . . .** because of some obstinate and rude behaviour which we took offence at (**conceived against him**)

OLIVIA	Ay, my lord, this same.	
	How now, Malvolio?	

| MALVOLIO | Madam, you have done me wrong, | 325 |
| | Notorious wrong. | |

| OLIVIA | Have I, Malvolio? No. | |

MALVOLIO Lady, you have. Pray you peruse that letter.
You must not now deny it is your hand;
Write from it, if you can, in hand or phrase;
Or say 't is not your seal nor your invention;   330
You can say none of this. Well, grant it then,
And tell me, in the modesty of honour,
Why you have given me such clear lights of favour,
Bade me come smiling and cross-gartered to you,
To put on yellow stockings, and to frown   335
Upon Sir Toby and the lighter people;
And, acting this in an obedient hope,
Why have you suffered me to be imprisoned,
Kept in a dark house, visited by the priest,
And made the most notorious geck and gull   340
That e'er invention played on? Tell me why.

OLIVIA Alas, Malvolio, this is not my writing,
Though, I confess, much like the character;
But, out of question, 't is Maria's hand;
And now I do bethink me, it was she   345
First told me thou wast mad; then cam'st in
     smiling,
And in such forms which here were presupposed
Upon thee in the letter. Prithee, be content;
This practice hath most shrewdly passed upon thee;
But when we know the grounds and authors of it,   350
Thou shalt be both the plaintiff and the judge
Of thine own cause.

FABIAN   Good madam, hear me speak,
And let no quarrel nor no brawl to come
Taint the condition of this present hour,
Which I have wondered at. In hope it shall not,   355
Most freely I confess, myself and Toby
Set this device against Malvolio here,
Upon some stubborn and uncourteous parts

5.1 A street near Olivia's house

Feste taunts Malvolio who leaves, vowing revenge. Orsino speaks to Viola about their coming marriage. Left alone, Feste sings a song.

Activities

Character review: Feste (6)

Feste's taunting speech (367–374) is the last thing he says before the song.

A To remind yourself why Feste says these lines and takes revenge in this way, (a) turn back to 1. 5 and act out lines 73–90; (b) re-read 2.5.142–145; then (c) act out lines 367–374 of this scene.

B 1. Re-read the activities you have completed on Feste (pages 22, 146 and 160) and then discuss how Feste should say his lines to Malvolio (367–374: 'Why, "some are born great . . .")'.

2. Act the speech viciously and sadistically; then act it as though you actually feel a little sorry for Malvolio. Compare your performances with other people's and discuss which interpretation best fits your view of Feste in the play as a whole.

C Discuss the ways in which Feste's taunting speech (a) most poignantly points out to Malvolio the folly of his aspirations; (b) shows Feste's need to let Malvolio know of his own part in the plot; (c) humiliates Malvolio by reminding him of his abject behaviour as a 'madman'; and (d) says something about the nature of revenge.

---

360 **importance** insistence

361 **In recompense whereof . . .** and, as a reward

362–365 **How with a . . .** The way in which it was conducted with a playful dislike (**sportful malice**), is more likely to cause you to laugh than take revenge, if you weigh up the injuries done on both sides.

366 **baffled thee** ridiculed you

369 **interlude** little play

370 **but that's all one** but that's not important

373–374 **and thus the whirligig of time . . .** and time, like a spinning-top, has brought us our revenge

376 **notoriously abused** shamefully mistreated

377 **entreat him to a peace** try to persuade him to make peace

379 **and golden time convents** when the time is right for something wonderful to take place

380 **solemn combination** a formal marriage ceremony

385 **his fancy's queen** his love's mistress

388 *A foolish thing . . .* 'a naughty child didn't matter' *(people used to let children get away with being naughty)*

390–392 But when I became a man, I found people's doors shut against me, as a knave and a thief.

We had conceived against him. Maria writ
The letter at Sir Toby's great importance;   360
In recompense whereof he hath married her.
How with a sportful malice it was followed,
May rather pluck on laughter than revenge,
If that the injuries be justly weighed
That have on both sides passed.   365

OLIVIA   Alas, poor fool, how have they baffled thee!

FESTE   Why, "some are born great, some achieve
greatness, and some have greatness thrown upon
them". I was one, sir, in this interlude; one Sir
Topas, sir; but that's all one. (*Imitating* MALVOLIO)   370
"By the Lord, fool, I am not mad." But do you
remember? "Madam, why laugh you at such a
barren rascal? An you smile not, he's gagged"; and
thus the whirligig of time brings in his revenges.

MALVOLIO   I'll be revenged on the whole pack of you.   375

                                           Exit.

OLIVIA   He hath been most notoriously abused.

DUKE   Pursue him, and entreat him to a peace.
He hath not told us of the captain yet;
When that is known, and golden time convents,
A solemn combination shall be made   380
Of our dear souls. Meantime, sweet sister,
We will not part from hence. Cesario, come;
For so you shall be, while you are a man;
But when in other habits you are seen,
Orsino's mistress, and his fancy's queen.   385

                         Exeunt all except FESTE.

FESTE (*Sings*)

    When that I was and a little tiny boy,
      With hey, ho, the wind and the rain;
    A foolish thing was but a toy,
      For the rain it raineth every day.

    But when I came to man's estate,   390
      With hey, ho, the wind and the rain;

5.1 A street near Olivia's house

Feste sings about the different stages in a person's life and concludes the play with a promise that whatever else happens, the actors will work hard to please the audience.

Activities

Character review: Malvolio (7)

As he exits, Malvolio cries: 'I'll be revenged on the whole pack of you.'

A Discuss what you think Malvolio would like to see happen to: Sir Toby and Maria; Feste; Olivia.

B Write a letter from any one of the characters listed in A, to one of the other characters, ten years after the end of the story told by the play, describing what has happened to yourself and to Malvolio.

C Write an entry for Malvolio's autobiography in which he recounts what has happened in the ten years following the humiliation in Olivia's house. Has he had his revenge on all or some of the characters? Is he now a better person with a clearer understanding, or merely an embittered man?

394–396 But when I got married, I could never get on by boastful bullying.

398–400 But when I grew old (*came unto my beds*), I was always coming home drunk to bed.

400 *toss-pots* drunkards

404 *But that's . . .* but that's not important now

404–405 *our play is done, And we'll strive to please you . . .* The actors will try hard (*strive*) to entertain the audience every time they come to the theatre. (This is the audience's cue to applaud.)

Act 5 Scene 1

'Gainst knaves and thieves men shut their gate,
  For the rain it raineth every day.

But when I came, alas, to wive,
  With hey, ho, the wind and the rain;   395
By swaggering could I never thrive,
  For the rain it raineth every day.

But when I came unto my beds,
  With hey, ho, the wind and the rain;
With toss-pots still had drunken heads,   400
  For the rain it raineth every day.

A great while ago the world begun,
  With hey, ho, the wind and the rain;
But that's all one, our play is done,
  And we'll strive to please you every day.   405

Exit.

in charge Toby & Maria   everybody obeys
older Orsino & Viola   husband
younger Sebastian & Olivia

5.1

Character review: Malvolio (8)

Malvolio's exit can leave the audience feeling extremely sad.

Philip Voss (1997) said: 'I want to howl and point to heaven – I shall try to pull my socks up and leave with dignity. I would like the audience to be heartbroken by him and to feel embarrassed. They must laugh – but then feel embarrassed.'

When Nigel Hawthorne played Malvolio (in the 1996 film), he left, in full view of the giggling servants, clutching his hair-piece, and was later seen departing from the house, carrying his suitcase.

A Draw a sketch which shows an utterly depressed Malvolio leaving the scene. Add thought-bubbles to all the other characters, showing what they feel (paying particular attention to Feste and Olivia).

B The interpretation chosen by the two actors referred to above does not have to be the only one. Alec McCowan's BBC TV Malvolio gave the impression that this is no more than a temporary setback, and that he will be back in power again.

List the evidence from the script which leads you to believe:
(a) that Malvolio is finished (think about the nature of his humiliation);
(b) that he will be back (think about how different Olivia's house will be in future: which new people will be there and which others will not).
Then act out lines 322–375.

C Look back at the notes you made about Malvolio's entrance, and also at activities on pages 120 and 158. Then write an essay: 'Malvolio: supercilious, trouble-maker and kill-joy, who is justly punished; or conscientious and loyal steward, cruelly victimised?'

In preparing your notes, consider how far an actor should strive to gain audience sympathy for Malvolio and what effect a sympathetic portrayal can have on the interpretation of the play as a whole.

Actors' interpretations (29): Feste's song

In the 1996 film, the director decided to show the different characters leaving Olivia's house as each verse was being sung: Sir Toby and Maria; Sir Andrew; Antonio; Malvolio; and Feste himself.

Discuss which leavers would suit each verse (and why) and what we might see them doing in a film version of *Twelfth Night*.

Actors interpretations (30): changing tones

A Contrasting tones. Find examples in Act 5 where the tone changes from comic to serious, or happy to sad, and discuss what it is that changes the tone in each case.

B Shifting tones. The critic Michael Mangan wrote about Act 5*: 'Its tone continually shifts, moment by moment, between intensity and frivolity, violence and tenderness, melodrama and downright farce, celebration and discord, wonder and harshness, laughter and melancholy.'

Discuss what is meant by each of these tones and find examples of them in Act 5.

Then draw a chart or diagram which represents this constant shifting of tone, including quotations from the script, or close reference to what happens.

C Dramatic effectiveness. Write a short essay which discusses and illustrates Michael Mangan's statement and considers the dramatic effectiveness of this constant shifting of tones. Look particularly at the final Act, including Feste's song, and consider why this might be a fitting ending to the play in performance

Character review: Fabian (2)

A When Orsino says 'Pursue him and entreat him to a peace', the character who offers to go after Malvolio is Fabian. Discuss what would make Fabian (i) a good choice; and (ii) a bad choice, if you wanted someone to persuade Malvolio to return and make peace with his tormentors.

B Discuss whether you agree with Fabian that their trick on Malvolio should really be a cause for laughter rather than revenge. From the script it is difficult to know whether Fabian himself really believes that. Act his speech (352–365), first as though he does believe what he says, then as though he doesn't.

C Fabian is an intriguing character. According to the script he does not appear until 2.5, but then Shakespeare gives him a significant role in 3.4 and important speeches at the end.

There is a theory that Shakespeare originally intended Feste to appear in 2.5 and 3.4 (see 2.3.169–170) but gave these scenes to a new character – Fabian, when he realised that he needed someone in Act 5 to explain calmly to Olivia what had happened and who was responsible.
1. Discuss the evidence in the script both for and against this theory.
2. Write about the function of Fabian in the plot of *Twelfth Night*.

* In *A Preface to Shakespeare's Comedies 1594–1603* (Longman, 1996, p 253).

Activities

Thinking about the play as a whole . . .

Actors' interpretations

1   **A**   *Filming the play*

Pick your favourite scene from the play and draw four or five frames of a storyboard, showing what the film version might look like.

B   *Staging a scene*

Pick a dramatic moment from the play and, using the plan on page 210, show how the moment might be staged, writing annotations to explain your decisions.

C   *Directing an extract*

Annotate a short scene or extract to show actors' movements, actions and reactions. Introduce it with a statement about the particular interpretation that you are aiming for (such as a sympathetic view of Malvolio in Act 5).

2   **A**   *Casting the play*

If you had the chance to direct a performance of *Twelfth Night*, which actors and actresses would you cast in the various roles? Make decisions about each character, explaining why you think the particular performer would be right for the part.

B   *A theatre programme*

Create a theatre programme for a production of *Twelfth Night*. This might include:

- a cast list with the names of the actors
- some background material (for example, on Twelfth Night celebrations in Shakespeare's time – see page 211; or articles on the wordplay or some of the major themes)
- details about Shakespeare and his plays.

C *A newspaper review*

Read the following review of a production of *Twelfth Night* by the Peter Hall Company in 1991:

A night of daylight and champagne

TWELFTH Night is about deception, about the difference between true love and its ego-centric counterfeits. Orsino is in love with love. Olivia is in love with grief, Malvolio is in love with himself. So say the textbooks, and up to a point they are obviously right.

But when you put it that way, half the magic evaporates. The play's moods are much too various to be summed up in a formula, its colours much too delicate; the lessons it teaches are less important than the world it creates, and its language races ahead – magnificently – of anything that the plot requires.

The first, the indispensable, things that we have a right to expect when we see Twelfth Night in the theatre are atmosphere and poetry. We must thrill to the willow cabin, or "day-light and champaign" or "thy mind is a very opal", as though we had never heard them before. We must be persuaded by Feste – by his tone, not just his sentiment – that "foolery, sir, does walk about the orb like the sun, it shines everywhere."

Peter Hall's new production at the Playhouse Theatre passes the basic test honourably and in many respects admirably. The Cavalier costumes and the Indian summer decor are good to look at; the lines, for the most part, are clearly and intelligently spoken.

There are weaknesses, however, Richard Garnett's Orsino is too mannered, especially in the early scenes – above all in his half smiling delivery of "If music be the food of love." Orsino's intoxication ought to be more powerful than that: you must feel the full enchantment before you can be properly disenchanted.

... Maria Miles's Viola, on the other hand, is delightful: she pulls off the essential trick of being entirely feminine and plausibly boyish at the same time ...

... Eric Porter is a strong, incisive Malvolio. He stands on his dignity, but the dignity is genuine. He is wonderfully convincing in the monologue where he persuades himself that he is about to achieve greatness; and you are left in no doubt by the end that he has been "notoriously abused".

When he is confined in a dark cell, all you can see are his hands, pleading through a partly opened trap-door. There is something truly terrible about the way Feste pushes back the flap at the end of the scene; and the effect is heightened by the way Sebastian promptly appears at the beginning of the next scene, with his "This is the air, that is the glorious sun."

John Gross, *Sunday Telegraph*

Write your own review, as a response to an actual theatre performance, or any one of the video versions that you have seen.

3 **A** *An advertisement*

Create a poster or newspaper advert for a new production of *Twelfth Night*, featuring some of your favourite actors. First look at some examples in

Activities

newspapers, to see how images are used and what written material is included.

 Video covers

Discuss these two covers of video versions of *Twelfth Night*.

- Which features of the story do they seem to be concentrating on?
- Which characters have they decided to highlight?
- How have they arranged the images?
- What text have they used to 'sell' the product?

Create a video cover for your own screen production of the play (which might feature some of the performers chosen for activity A).

C *A display*

Put together a classroom display on *Twelfth Night*, which would be interesting for a younger class approaching the play for the first time. Include:

- the props that you have created (Maria's forged letter, Sir Andrew's challenge . . .)
- any drawings that you have done (stage designs, storyboards . . .)
- other background work (Malvolio's report to Olivia; the 'willow cabin' collage; the 'Wanted' poster on Antonio; the Illyria tourism article; the drawing of the fierce Sir Andrew; the video covers . . .)

- anything else you can think of (Malvolio's letter written in prison; a poster advertising the play . . .)
- things that you have collected from productions (production postcards, programmes, reviews . . .).

You will need to write some introductory material, explaining what the play is about and how the various elements of the display tie in.

Character reviews

4 Character profiles

Some actors write systematic notes about the characters they are preparing to play. Draw up a Character Profile form on a word-processor and then fill it in for any characters you are working on. Headings might be:

NAME:
SOCIAL POSITION:
SUPER-OBJECTIVE: (the character's overriding aim, which drives them on: e.g. 'to marry Olivia')
LINE OF ACTION: (the practical things they must do to achieve that aim: e.g. 'send her love messages via Cesario . . .')
OBSTACLES AGAINST IT: (e.g. 'Olivia is refusing to see me because . . .')
WHAT THE CHARACTER SAYS ABOUT HERSELF/HIMSELF:
WHAT OTHER CHARACTERS SAY ABOUT HER/HIM:
IMPRESSION ON FIRST APPEARANCE:
RELATIONSHIPS WITH OTHERS:
OTHER INFORMATION:
(and you might also add an ANIMAL – see page 68)

5 Character review: Malvolio

Think about how much sympathy you have for Malvolio, and how much you would want an audience to have if you were directing the play. First re-read the activities on pages 58, 82, 88, 120, 144, 158, 186, 188 and the key scenes: 1.5; 2.2; 2.3; 2.5; 3.4; 4.2; 5.1.

Ⓐ *Laughter and sympathy*

Pick one of the scenes in which Malvolio appears. List (a) all the things which make you laugh at him; and (b) the things which give you sympathy for him.

Activities

B *A sympathy graph*

First discuss whether you feel that the revenge taken against Malvolio is too harsh and his treatment too cruel. Then draw a graph. On the x axis, mark at least ten points in the story of Malvolio (including his first and last appearances). On the y axis, draw a scale of 0–10, according to how much sympathy you feel for him (10 being the highest). Plot your graph and then compare it with other people's, discussing the differences in your responses. Finally write an essay entitled 'How much sympathy I feel for Malvolio'.

C *A comic character*

Write an essay exploring the opportunities offered to an actor for humour in the role of Malvolio.

6 Character review: Feste

Feste is an intriguing character. Re-read the activities on pages 22, 26, 32, 146, 160, 184 and the key scenes: 1.5; 2.3; 2.4; 3.1; 4.1; 4.2; 5.1.

A *Feste's role*

What exactly does Feste do in this story? Look back through the play and draw a diagram or flow-chart which shows (a) what he actually does in the two plots (the Olivia-Viola-Orsino triangle and the fooling of Malvolio); and (b) how he is connected to the various characters.

B *Feste's autobiography*

Write the chapter of Feste's autobiography which records the days in Olivia's household covered in *Twelfth Night*. Remember to include only your own view of events (you were not present when Malvolio found the letter, for example), opinions on characters and judgements about the treatment of Malvolio. A really interesting chapter will be written in a style that reflects Feste's love of words.

C *A god-like figure?*

In the 1996 film, Ben Kingsley's Feste saw Viola landing on the shores of Illyria and disguising herself. That meant that he was almost a 'god-like' figure, who knew throughout what was going on. Discuss which aspects of the play and which parts of the script would support this interpretation and what could be done in a film to bring out his knowledge and awareness.

7 Character review: Viola

To recap on the central character in the play, re-read the activities on pages 40, 48, 72, 86, 134, 136, 176 and the key scenes: 1.2; 1.4; 1.5; 2.2; 2.4; 3.1; 3.4; 5.1.

Ⓐ *Viola's qualities*

What would you say Viola's strongest qualities were? List as many as you can and find moments in the play to support each one. First think about the meanings of the following and see in what ways they relate to Viola: resourcefulness, loyalty, courage, love, patience, intelligence, wit, straightforwardness, dignity.

Ⓑ *A reference for Cesario*

Imagine you are Orsino, writing a reference for Cesario, who has applied for a post in another Duke's court. Write about 'his' qualities (bearing in mind that you are not aware of all the qualities listed in activity A) and give evidence from what you have seen 'him' do, to support each one. Assume that you are writing before you realise that Olivia has fallen in love with Cesario. Try to make the reference rich in dramatic irony (see page 100).

Ⓒ *A favourite heroine*

Write an essay discussing the following question: 'What would you say it was about Viola which made her many people's favourite among Shakespeare's heroines?'

8 Character review: Orsino

Although an important character, Orsino does not appear very frequently. Re-read the activities on pages 18, 38, 44, 66, 70, 178 and the key scenes: 1.1; 1.4; (1.5. 261–265); 2.4; 5.1.

Ⓐ *Orsino's attractions*

Which qualities of Orsino's make Viola fall in love with him, in your opinion? You might like to re-read 1.1; 1.4; 1.5 (261–265); and 2.4.

Ⓑ *Descriptions of Orsino*

Write two descriptions of Orsino, one written by Feste, the other by Viola. Concentrate particularly on the different sides of the man that each one sees. Look particularly at 1.4; 2.4; and 5.1.

Activities

⊙ *Views of Orsino*

Clive Wood, who played Orsino in 1994, said: 'I've always had this kind of preconception of Orsino, which I think many people have, as a melancholic romantic flopping around on cushions. But when the part was offered to me and I was reading the play, my immediate reaction was the opposite: Orsino is an absolutely tormented man who's got so many demons.' Write an essay in which you discuss the different ways in which Orsino can be played: as a genuinely tormented lover, a self-indulgent poseur, an immature and aimless aristocrat with time on his hands ... What does Feste mean, when he says that Orsino's mind is 'a very opal' (2.4.75), and how important is that judgement to your view of the Duke?

9 Character review: Olivia

Olivia is a figure much discussed by other characters in the play. Re-read the activities on pages 4, 24, 42 and the key scenes: (1.1.32–38); 1.5; 3.1; 3.4; 4.1; 4.3; 5.1.

A *Other people's comments*

Make a list of what other people say about Olivia. In particular, re-read the first act of the play, listing who says what about her. What does she reveal about herself in 1.5; 3.1; and 3.4?

B *Her own feelings*

Write an entry for Olivia's diary in which she weighs up the rival attractions of Orsino, Sir Andrew Aguecheek and Cesario.

⊙ *Strengths and weaknesses*

Write an essay in which you compare Olivia's weaknesses (for example her impetuosity and possibly excessive melancholy) with her strengths (such as her perceptive analysis of Malvolio). What is your own opinion of her, on balance?

10 Character review: Sir Toby Belch

Re-read the activities on pages 18 and 148 and the key scenes: 1.3; 1.5; 2.3; 2.5; 3.1; 3.2; 3.4; 4.1; 4.2; 5.1.

A *His statements*

Find six of these quotations of Sir Toby's (including the first and the last) and discuss what each reveals about him. (For example, the first one says something about his attitude to Olivia and his love of drinking.)

I'll drink to her as long as there is a passage in my throat . . .
Wherefore are these things hid?
I hate it as an unfilled can.
Am I not of her blood?
Dost thou think, because thou art virtuous, there shall be no more cakes
  and ale?
She's a beagle, true-bred, and one that adores me . . .
O! for a stone-bow . . .
I could marry this wench for this device.
. . . challenge me the count's youth to fight with him . . .
I have been dear to him, lad . . .
Come, we'll have him in a dark room, and bound . . .
Now will not I deliver his letter . . .
Marry, I'll ride your horse as well as I ride you.
Nay, if you be an undertaker, I am for you.
I would we were well rid of this knavery.
Will you help? An ass-head, and a coxcomb, and a knave . . .!

B *Maria's view*

Fabian reveals at the end of the play that, as a reward for the plot against Malvolio, Sir Toby has married Maria. Write a letter from Maria to her sister, in which she describes the man who has proposed to her and discusses the reasons for and against marrying him.

C *A mixed character*

Discuss the opinion that 'Despite Sir Toby's jolliness and wit, we cannot warm to a character who manipulates and exploits the innocent Sir Andrew Aguecheek, and who reveals other unpleasant aspects of character, such as a tendency to violence.'

11 Character review: Maria, Sir Andrew, Sebastian and Antonio

Re-read the activities and the key scenes:

- Maria: 1.3; 1.5; 2.3; 2.5; 3.2; 3.4; 4.2; and pages 14, 159
- Sir Andrew: 1.3; 2.3; 2.5; 3.1; 3.2; 3.4; 4.1; 5.1; and pages 16, 86, 124, 126
- Sebastian: 2.1; 3.3; 4.1; 4.3; 5.1; and pages 46, 142
- Antonio: 2.1; 3.3; 3.4; 5.1; and pages 46, 108, 130, 164

Activities

(A) *Selecting quotations*

Pick one of these characters and pick out five quotations, like those in question 10A, which represent the character's qualities. Then ask your partner to find the quotations and discuss what each one reveals about the character.

(B) *Acting opportunities*

What opportunities are there for an actress playing Maria or an actor playing Sir Andrew Aguecheek, Sebastian or Antonio? Pick one character, look at the scenes in which she or he appears and describe what satisfaction and enjoyment exists in playing the part. (You could write this from the actor's point of view, using his or her 'voice'.)

(C) *Contributions*

Twelfth Night has one of the smallest casts of any Shakespeare play. Write an essay explaining how any one or more of the following contributes to the plots, and in what other ways the character is interesting: Maria, Sir Andrew Aguecheek, Sebastian, Antonio.

Shakespeare's language

12 **(A)** *A poster*

Look back through the play and find an example of each of the following:

- wordplay (look at the activities on pages 90, 166)
- imagery (see pages 80, 98, 139, 166)
- dramatic irony (see page 100).

Create a poster for the classroom with the title 'Shakespeare's language in *Twelfth Night*', which includes the three examples, with a brief written account and a drawing which explains how each one works.

(B) *A collage*

Look back at the activities to do with imagery (pages 80, 98, 139, 166) and write an essay explaining how the images in the play help to convey characters' attitudes to love.

ⓒ *A reference work, wordplay and imagery*

Collect together the written material that you have compiled:

- the glossary of changing meanings
- examples of wordplay
- examples of dramatic irony
- references to classical myths and legends
- the imagery databases
- any other notes or background materials.

(a) Using a word-processor, compile a reference work which would be useful to anybody studying the play at Key Stage 3.

(b) Write an essay on one of the following: either the importance of wordplay in reinforcing the ambiguities of characters' behaviour; or the range of imagery in the play and ways in which it affects our understanding of characters and themes.

Themes

13 A theme is a subject which seems to arise at several times in the play so that we receive different perspectives on it. Themes in *Twelfth Night* include the following (with some key scenes and references):

- Time: 2.2.39–40; 2.3 (Feste's song); 5.1.374
- Love: 1.1; 1.2; 1.4; 1.5.91, 255–314; 2.1.47–48; 2.2.16–38; 2.4; 3.1; 3.4.364–368; 5.1
- Madness: 1.5.133–140, 201; 2.5.193–195; 3.4; 4.1.26; 4.2; 4.3; 5.1.94, 275–310
- Appearance and reality: 1.2; 2.2.17, 26–27 . . .; 3.4.371–375; 4.2; 5.1. Viola's disguise; Malvolio's pretended Puritanism; the fake letter; Toby's feigned friendship for Aguecheek; the duel.

Ⓐ *A theme collage*

Find as many references as you can to either Time, Love, Madness, or Appearance and reality in the play and create a collage which illustrates the variety of views on the subject. For example, a collage on Time might include a knot (for 2.2.39–40) and a child's spinning-top (for 5.1.374). Add the relevant quotations to the illustrations and display your collage.

Activities

B *Discussing the theme*

(a) Time: Discuss how far you agree with Zoe Wanamaker's view of the play that it is 'a story about time, and growing up'. Think about:

- the things that can only be sorted out by time
- what people say about time in the play
- which characters particularly have to 'grow up' as the story progresses (especially in their attitudes to love).

(b) Love: Look back at the activity on Love (page 2) and write two paragraphs contrasting any two of the 'loves' in the play. State what it is that distinguishes them from each other.

(c) Madness: Bearing in mind the following facts (and others that you can think of), discuss how far you would agree that madness seems to be a widespread 'disease' in Illyria:

- according to Feste, Sir Toby is a 'madman' because of his drink (1.5. 139)
- Orsino thinks Antonio's words are 'madness' (5.1.94)
- Olivia says, 'If you be not mad, be gone' (1.5.201)
- Malvolio suffers from 'midsummer madness' (3.4.54)
- and asks 'My masters, are you mad ...?' (2.3.83)
- Sebastian wonders 'Are all the people mad?' (4.1.26)
- then whether he or Olivia are mad (4.3.1–16)
- there is a possibility that Malvolio will be driven 'mad indeed' (3.4.135).

(d) Appearance and reality: Draw up two columns: How things appear to be; and How things really are. Look back at the activities on pages 96, 134 and 140, and at other moments in the play, and complete the chart. Include the deceptions that people intentionally practise upon others, the examples of people being deceived about themselves and the moments when disguise is used.

C *Analysing the theme*

Write about one of the following, first re-reading the activities on the relevant pages:

- The importance of the theme of time in *Twelfth Night*.
- The different aspects of love and friendship presented in *Twelfth Night*. Does there seem to you to be any overall 'message' that can be read from the play?
- The theme of madness. Discuss in particular the view that it is 'the dominant metaphor of the play' (Michael Mangan).
- Disguise and deception, appearance and reality (including self-deception) in *Twelfth Night*.

General questions

Although most characters seem happy at the end of the play, there are clearly some who are not, and many productions like to bring out this darker side to the comedy.

14 **A** *Who might be unhappy?*

Malvolio is obviously unhappy, but so too (in some productions) are Sir Andrew, Feste and Antonio. Discuss the reasons each of these last three characters might have for being unhappy at the end of the play. How happy do you think Maria and Sir Toby are?

B *Reporting their fates*

Create the front page of the *Illyria Sun* (a tabloid newspaper), for the day after the double wedding. Together with a spread on the wedding itself (with quotations from appropriate characters), add small articles at the bottom, reporting what has happened to Malvolio (and possibly Antonio or Feste or Sir Andrew).

C *Dark and serious elements*

Write an essay which discusses this statement by Stephen Boxer, who played Feste in 1997: 'If you play the dark and serious elements of plays they always become funnier. If you just play the humour, personally I don't find it funny. I've seen this play done as a pantomime and there's more to it than that. In the romantic scene when Feste sings "Come away, come away, death" to Orsino, I hope the paradox [apparent contradiction] of love coupled with death is both amusing and profound.'

In your essay, discuss what the darker elements might be. Think, for example, about the treatment of Malvolio, Sir Andrew and Antonio, as well as the view of the world that Feste has.

15 **Foolery**

What are the arguments for considering 'foolery' to be a significant theme of *Twelfth Night*? Think about Feste's role particularly.

Background to Shakespeare

Do some research in an encyclopedia or CD-ROM to find out more about the background features highlighted in **bold**.
There are also activities for additional research.

Shakespeare's England

Shakespeare lived during a period called the **Renaissance**: a time when extraordinary changes were taking place, especially in the fields of religion, politics, science, language and the arts. He wrote during the reigns of **Elizabeth I** and **James I**.

Religion and politics

- In the century following the **Reformation** and England's break with Rome in the 1530s, people in Shakespeare's England began to view the world and their own place in it very differently.

- Queen Elizabeth restored the **Protestant religion** in England, begun under her father Henry VIII.

- England had become a proud and independent nation, and a leading military and trading power, especially after the defeat of the **Spanish Armada** in 1588.

- There were divisions in the Protestant Church, with extremist groups such as the **Puritans** (see page 211), disapproving of much of what they saw in society and the Church.

- James I succeeded Elizabeth in 1603. He was a Scot, interested in witchcraft, and a supporter of the theatre, who fought off the treasonous attempt of the **Gunpowder Plot** in 1605.

- People began to question traditional beliefs about rank and social order – ideas that some people should be considered superior simply because they were born into wealthy families; or that those in power should always be obeyed without question.

Discuss how these ideas can be seen reflected in *Twelfth Night*.

- As trade became increasingly important, it was not only the nobility who could become wealthy. People could move around the country more easily and a competitive **capitalist economy** developed.

Science and discovery

- Scientists began to question traditional authorities (the accepted ideas handed down from one generation to the next) and depended instead upon their own observation of the world, especially after the development of instruments such as the telescope. **Galileo** came into conflict with the Church for claiming that the Earth was not the centre of the universe.

Check how Shakespeare reflects the arguments which were current in his time about the soul and reincarnation in Feste's conversation with the imprisoned Malvolio.

- Explorers and traders brought back new produce, such as spices and silks, and created great excitement in the popular imagination for stories of distant lands and their peoples.

Language

- The more traditional scholars still regarded **Latin** as the only adequate language for scholarly discussion and writing (and liked it because it also prevented many 'uncultured' people from understanding philosophy, medicine, etc.).
- A new interest in the **English language** came with England's growing importance and sense of identity.
- The Protestants favoured a personal relationship with God, which meant being able to read the Bible themselves (rather than letting priests interpret it for them). This led to the need for a good version in English, and **The Authorised Version of the Bible** (the 'King James Bible') was published in 1611.
- **Grammar schools** sprang up after the Reformation which increased literacy (but mostly among males in the middle and upper classes, and mainly in London).

- The invention of the **printing press** in the 1450s had led to more people having access to information and new ideas – not just the scholars.
- The English language began to be standardised in this period (into **Standard English**), but it was still very flexible and there was less insistence on following rules than there is nowadays.
- There was an enormous expansion in **vocabulary**, which affected every area of daily life: crafts, sciences, technology, trade, philosophy, food . . .
- English vocabulary was enriched by numerous **borrowings** from other languages. Between 1500 and 1650, over 10,000 new words entered the language (though many later fell out of use). Some 'purists' (who disliked change) opposed the introduction of new words.

Use a dictionary to find where the words for common foods came from: coffee, tea, tomato, chocolate, potato . . .

- Shakespeare therefore lived through a time when the English vocabulary was expanding amazingly and the grammar was still flexible, a time when people were intensely excited by language.

Shakespeare's plays reflect this fascination for words. Do some research to find examples of: Mercutio's wit in *Romeo and Juliet*; Dogberry's slip-ups in *Much Ado About Nothing*; Shylock's fatal bond and Portia's 'escape clause' in *The Merchant of Venice*; the puzzling oracle in *The Winter's Tale*; and Bottom's problems with words ('I see a voice!') in *A Midsummer Night's*

Plays and playhouses

The theatre was a very popular form of entertainment in Shakespeare's time, with audiences drawn from all classes of people. The theatre buildings and the companies of actors were different from what we are used to today.

The theatres

- The professional theatre was based exclusively in London, which had around 200,000 inhabitants in 1600.

- It was often under attack from the **Puritan**-dominated Guildhall, which wanted to abolish the theatres totally because, in their opinion, they encouraged sinful behaviour.
- Acting companies first performed in the courtyards of coaching inns, in the halls of great houses, in churches, at markets and in the streets. The first outdoor playhouse was The Red Lion, built in c.1567 (when Shakespeare was three).
- By 1600, there were eleven public outdoor theatres, including **the Rose**, the Swan and the Globe (Shakespeare's theatre).
- **Shakespeare's Globe** opened in 1599 on Maiden Lane, Bankside, and was destroyed by fire during a performance of *Henry VIII* in 1613. (No one was killed, but a bottle of ale was needed to put out a fire in a man's breeches!). See pages 207–209.
- Some outdoor theatres held audiences of up to 3,000.
- Standing room was one penny; the gallery twopence; the 'Lords' Room' threepence; and it was more expensive still to sit on the stage. This was at a time when a joiner (skilled carpenter) might earn 6s to 8s (72 to 96 pence) per week. By 1614, it was 6d ($2^1/_2$ pence) for the newly opened indoor Hope theatre.

Work out whether it was cheaper or more expensive to go to the theatre in Shakespeare's time than it is today. (To do the comparison, you will need to find out (a) how much the cheapest and most expensive tickets are at the Royal Shakespeare Theatre, Stratford-upon-Avon, for example; and (b) what a skilled worker might earn nowadays.)

- Outdoor theatre performances usually started about 2 pm or 3 pm (there was no artificial light).
- The season started in September, through to the beginning of Lent; then from after Easter to early summer. (Theatres were closed during outbreaks of **the plague**: 11,000 died of the plague in summer 1593 and the theatres remained almost completely closed until 1594.) Some companies went on summer tours, playing in inns, etc.
- The majority of theatres were closed during the **Civil War**, in 1642 (and most of the playhouses were demolished by 1656).
- There were some indoor theatres (called 'private' or 'hall' theatres) such as the **Blackfriars**, which was used up to 1609 almost exclusively by child actors (the minimum entrance fee of sixpence indicates a wealthier audience). Plays developed which were more suited to the more intimate atmosphere, with the stage illuminated by artificial lighting.
- The star actor **Richard Burbage** and his brother Cuthbert had the licence

of the Blackfriars from 1596 and Shakespeare's later plays were performed there.

Work out from page 224 which of Shakespeare's plays might have been written with the indoor Blackfriars theatre in mind.

The actors

- In 1572 parliament passed an Act 'For the Punishment of Vagabonds'. As actors were classed as little better than wandering beggars, this Act required them to be attached to a theatre company and have the patronage (financial support and protection) of someone powerful. This meant that companies had to keep on the right side of patrons and make sure they didn't offend the Master of the Revels, who was responsible for **censorship**.

- Major companies in Shakespeare's time included the Admiral's Men and the Queen's Men. **The Lord Chamberlain's Men** (the group that Shakespeare joined, later known as **the King's Men** when James came to the throne) was formed in 1594 and was run by shareholders (called 'the housekeepers').

- The Burbages held 50 per cent of the shares of the company; the remaining 50 per cent was divided mainly between the actors, including Shakespeare himself, who owned about 10 per cent – which helped to earn him a comfortable regular income.

Acting

- There was very little rehearsal time, with several plays 'in repertory' (being performed) in any given period.

- We don't actually know about the style of acting, but modern, naturalistic, low-key acting was not possible on the Globe stage. At the same time, Shakespeare appears to be mocking over-the-top delivery in at least two of his plays.

Read *Hamlet* 3.2 (Hamlet's first three speeches to the First Player) and *A Midsummer Night's Dream* (especially Act 5).

- Actors certainly needed to be aware of their relationship with the audience: there must have been plenty of direct contact. In a daylight theatre there can be no pretence that the audience is not there.

Publishing

- Plays were not really regarded as 'literature' in Shakespeare's lifetime, and so the playwright would not have been interested in publishing his plays in book form.
- Some of Shakespeare's plays were, however, originally printed in cheap 'quarto' (pocket-sized) editions. Some were sold officially (under an agreement made between the theatre company and the author), and some pirated (frequently by the actors themselves who had learned most of the script by heart).
- In 1623, seven years after Shakespeare's death, two of his close friends, John Heminges and Henry Condell, collected together the most reliable versions of the plays and published them in a larger size volume known as **the First Folio**. This included eighteen plays which had never before appeared in print, and eighteen more which had appeared in quarto editions. Only *Pericles* was omitted from the plays which make up what we nowadays call Shakespeare's 'Complete Works' (unless we count plays such as The Noble Kinsmen, for which Shakespeare is known to have written some scenes).

Much of the information in these sections comes from Michael Mangan, *A Preface to Shakespeare's Comedies: 1594–1603* Longman, 1996

The Globe theatre

No one knows precisely what Shakespeare's Globe theatre looked like, but we do have a number of clues:

- a section of the foundations has been unearthed and provides an idea of the size and shape of the outside walls
- the foundations of the Rose, a theatre near the Globe, were excavated in 1988–89

Using much of the evidence available, a reconstruction of Shakespeare's Globe theatre has been built in London, not far from the site of the original building.

Background to Shakespeare

- a Dutch visitor to Shakespeare's London, called Johannes de Witt, saw a play in the Swan Theatre and made a sketch of the interior.

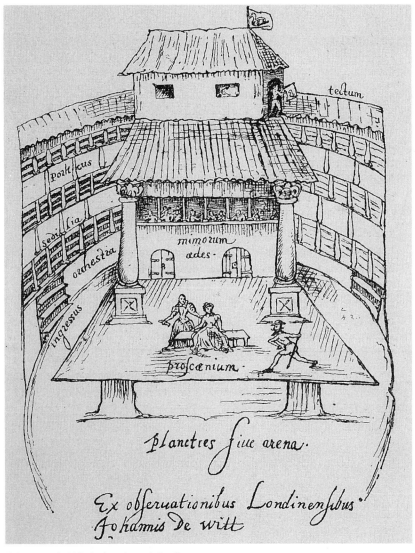

Johannes de Witt's drawing of the Swan

Ⓐ *The facts*

From what you can learn from these photographs:

- Roughly what shape is the theatre, looked at from above?
- How many storeys does it have?
- In which areas can the audience (a) stand, and (b) sit?
- What is behind the stage?
- How much scenery and lighting are used?
- What other details can you pick out which seem to make the Globe different from an indoor theatre (which has a stage at one end, similar to many school assembly halls)?
- Find a copy of Shakespeare's *Henry V* and read the opening speech (by the Chorus) to see what phrase Shakespeare himself famously used to describe the shape of an earlier theatre, the Curtain.

Ⓑ *Using the stage*

Copy the plan on page 210. Then, using the staging guidelines provided, sketch or mark characters as they might appear at crucial moments in *Twelfth Night* (such as Malvolio's entrances in 2.3 and 5.1 or Sebastian's in 5.1).

Ⓒ *The actor–audience relationship*

- In what ways is the design of Shakespeare's Globe ideally suited to the performance of his plays?
- How might the open stage and the balcony be useful? (Refer to moments in *Twelfth Night* or other Shakespeare plays that you know.)
- What do you think would be the most interesting features of the way in which Shakespeare's actors – and those on the reconstructed Globe today – might relate to and interact with the audience? (Which moments in *Twelfth Night* seem to require a performance in which the audience are very close to the actors, for example?)

Background to Shakespeare

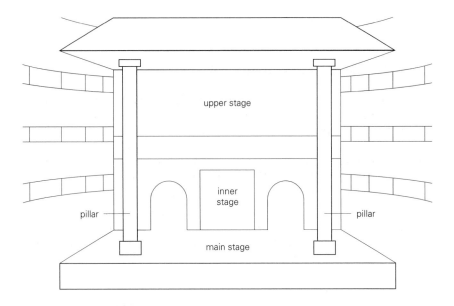

Above: front on view of the stage, as seen by the audience.

Below: bird's-eye view of the stage for positioning of characters.

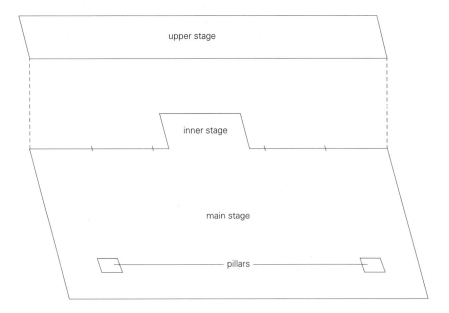

The social background

Twelfth Night celebrations

- For many centuries Christian communities have celebrated the feast of **Epiphany** – the time when the infant Jesus was first presented to the Magi (the Three Wise Men) – twelve days after his birth on Christmas Day.
- In Shakespeare's time, this whole period from 25 December to 6 January was given over to 'Yuletide revels' – a time of feasting and celebration which possibly dates back to the Roman **Saturnalia**.
- In some private houses a **'Lord of Misrule'** was elected, usually from among the servants, who was given authority to organise the festivities.
- During this extended partying, it was traditional to play tricks on people, and it was understood that, for a while, the usual master–servant relationships were turned on their heads.
- This was a period of carnival in which, typically:
  - (a) people might give way to bodily pleasures of all kinds (drinking too much, indulging in sex, over-eating . . .);
  - (b) language itself seemed to run riot (with jokes, nonsense and wit);
  - (c) the traditional hierarchies (the lord and lady 'at the top'; the servants in various ranks beneath them) were temporarily overthrown.
- Twelfth Night itself marked the end of these festivities – and was therefore a signal that the 'misrule' was over and that the traditional hierarchies would once again be in place.

Discuss the appropriateness of the title of this play.

Puritans

- The term 'Puritan' was used about a particular sect of Protestants who took a very hard-line view of what they considered to be sin and disorder in Shakespeare's England, and saw it as their duty to resist it through preaching and in their own behaviour.
- They were a powerful and influential group, prominent among the growing middle classes, and dominated London's Guildhall (which made rules for the City).

211

Background to Shakespeare

- Among other measures, they wanted to close the theatres which they considered to be the hot-beds of sin and all manner of vices.
- Playwrights therefore hated the Puritans and mocked them as being hypocrites who claimed to be pure and religious enemies of sin, but who instead (a) complained about simple pleasures – symbolised by 'cakes and ale' (2.3.112), and (b) sometimes used religion as a 'front' to further their own ambitions and secret vices.
- When Maria says of Malvolio that 'sometimes he is a kind of puritan', but that, in reality he is 'a time-pleaser', she perhaps means that he behaves like a Puritan when it suits him, but that he does not genuinely subscribe to Puritanism as a faith (2.3.136, 143).

Do some research to find out (a) which major historical event took place some forty years after *Twelfth Night* was first performed; (b) what connection it had with Puritans; and (c) what happened to the theatres during that time. Then discuss how Malvolio's parting words 'I'll be revenged on the whole pack of you' came to take on a very sinister edge which Shakespeare could not have known about.

Fools

- In the cast list based on the First Folio, Feste is described as a 'clown'; in the play he is usually 'fool', but Curio calls him a 'jester' (2.4.11); Feste describes himself as a 'corrupter of words' (3.1.37).
- A 'jester' was originally somebody who sang songs or told stories of great heroic deeds, rather like a minstrel. By Shakespeare's time, the word seems to have been used for a comic who also sang songs.
- The term 'clown' often appears in Shakespeare's plays for characters like the young shepherd in *The Winter's Tale* – country boys who did not know the ways of the city; but it was more generally applied to any comic character, such as the gravediggers in *Hamlet*.
- Many medieval lords kept 'fools' who were sometimes mentally handicapped (something which today would be seen as a cruel and inhuman source of amusement).
- The fools in Shakespeare's plays are clearly intelligent men with a flair for words who put on an act of folly to entertain their masters and mistresses; but Shakespeare's audiences would still have made the link with the earlier kind of 'natural' fool (see 1.3.29) and the theme of 'madness' generally.

- The fool was in the strange position of being able to say what he liked to his lord or lady, while remaining totally dependent upon them for his living (rather like an Elizabethen actor who needed the support of a patron).
- Characters such as Feste in *Twelfth Night*, Touchstone in *As You Like It* and the Fool in *King Lear* are constantly forcing us to ask the question 'Who is the real fool here?'

Discuss exactly what power Feste has, and where his power ends.

Social class

- During the Middle Ages, power and wealth had been exclusively in the hands of a minority of people and was handed down from generation to generation within the same family. The increase of trade saw the rise of the middle classes, a new group who were acquiring wealth through their own skill, energy and enterprise.

Write the names of all the characters on slips of paper. Then think carefully about the social class or rank of each one and place the slips in order, with the spaces between them representing the size of the social gulfs. Base your decisions upon the ways the characters interact: there are no definite answers to (a) the difference in rank between Orsino and Olivia; (b) where to place Malvolio, who is a steward but also a 'gentleman' (4.2.85; 5.1.275); (c) what rank Maria is ('chambermaid' – 1.3.50; or 'gentlewoman' – 1.5.166–167); and (d) how Feste fits in.

Shakespeare's verse

Metre

Every word we use in English can be described according to where the heavy stress falls. For example, these three words (from 1.1.1–7) have their heavy stress on the first syllable: **mu**sic, **sur**feiting, **app**etite; while in these the heavy stress is on the second syllable: exc**ess**, ag**ain**, en**ough**.

All Shakespeare's verse has a pattern of light and heavy stresses running through it, known as the metre. You can hear the metre if you read these lines out loud, over-emphasising the heavily stressed syllables:

- If **mu**sic **be** the **food** of **love**, play **on** (1.1.1)
- That **strain** ag**ain**! it **had** a **dy**ing **fall** (1.1.4)
- O, **when** mine **eyes** did **see** O**li**via **first** (1.1.18)

No actor would ever perform the lines in that monotonous way, but they would certainly be aware that the metre was always there, helping to give the verse form and structure.

Sometimes, to point out that a syllable which does not carry a heavy stress in modern English is stressed in Shakespeare's line of verse, it will be accented, like this:

- For which, if I be lapséd in this place (3.3.36)

(a) Mark the heavy stresses in that line of Antonio's (3. 3. 36).
(b) The four lines above are all totally regular in their metre: what do you notice about: (i) the pattern of short and heavy stresses; (ii) the number of syllables?

Varying the metre

Most of the lines in Shakespeare's plays are not as regular as the four quoted above. In fact, most will have an irregular stress pattern, like this one, where the irregularity perhaps helps the actor to convey Orsino's troubled emotions:

- **Stea**ling and **giv**ing **od**our. En**ough**! no **more** (1.1.7)

Occasionally a line will contain an extra syllable (11 rather than 10):

- O **spir**it of **love**! how **quick** and **fresh** art **thou** (1.1.9)

Here the actor can either try to deliver 'O spirit' as though it were two syllables (making it a regular line), or emphasise the slowness of the phrase, perhaps underlining its importance.

Also unusually, the line might be a syllable short, and this can give a very abrupt impression, especially when it comes at the end of a speech:

- And lasting in her sad remembrance (1.1.31)

Some lines really stand out, because they are clearly short:

- 'What is your parentage?' (1.5.292)

A collection of heavy stresses together can add emphasis, especially in a 9-syllable line:

- Her **sweet** per**fec**tions, with **one self king**! (1.1.38)

Dividing the line into feet

Just as music has a number of beats in a bar, so Shakespeare's verse has five 'feet' in a complete line. A five-foot line is called a 'pentameter' (pent = five; meter = measure).

A single foot can contain syllables from different words, and any one word can be broken up by the foot divisions:

- That, **not** I with**stan** I -ding **thy** I ca**pa** I -city (1.1.10)

This is why a single line of verse is sometimes set out rather oddly in different lines of print, if it is shared between two or more characters:

CURIO   Will you go hunt, my lord?
DUKE   What, Curio?
CURIO   The hart. (1.1.16)

Iambic pentameter

A foot which contains an unstressed syllable followed by a stressed one (the standard 'beat': dee-**dum**) is called an 'iamb'. Verse which has five iambs per line as its standard rhythm is called an 'iambic pentameter'.

Iambic pentameter which does not rhyme is also sometimes known as 'blank verse'.

(a) Bearing in mind that the iambic pentameter line goes: dee-**dum**, dee-**dum**, dee-**dum**, dee-**dum**, dee-**dum**, make up some of your own 'Shakespearean' verse (perhaps based on one of the themes of the play).
(b) Copy out the following lines from 1.1 and divide them into five feet; then mark the heavy stresses: lines 11, 15, 26, 34 and 40.

Rhyme

Although there are some passages of rhyming verse in Shakespeare's plays (and, of course, many songs), he usually reserves it for the ends of scenes, where a 'rhyming couplet' can have the effect of rounding things off, as it does in 1.1.

Find the other scenes which end with a rhyming couplet and discuss what the effect might be in each case.

Verse and prose

It is never totally clear why Shakespeare chooses to write some scenes, or passages, in verse, and others in prose. Although there are many examples where the more serious scenes, involving great passions, are in verse while those about ordinary people and comedy are in prose, there are also significant examples throughout Shakespeare's plays where this is not the case.

In 1.5, Viola and Olivia speak lines 170–240 in prose and then switch to verse for 241–291; in 2.2, Viola talks to Malvolio in prose, but speaks her soliloquy (a speech in which a character utters their thoughts to the audience) in verse; in 5.1, Viola addresses Sir Andrew in verse and he replies in prose (5.1.182–189).

Discuss whether any rules can be drawn up for the use of verse and prose in *Twelfth Night*. Look, for example, at (a) soliloquies; (b) 'comic' and 'romantic' exchanges; (c) which characters use mainly one or the other; (d) the way the dialogue keeps changing from verse to prose and back again in 5.1.

The plot of *Twelfth Night*

There are really three interwoven plots in *Twelfth Night*; they involve:

- the 'love-triangle' of Viola-Orsino-Olivia
- the gulling of Malvolio
- Antonio's friendship for Sebastian.

Act 1

1.1: Orsino, Duke of Illyria, is in love with the Countess Olivia, but she consistently refuses to entertain thoughts of marriage as she is mourning the death of her brother.

1.2: After a shipwreck, Viola is helped ashore by a Captain, who reassures her that her brother Sebastian might not be drowned, and promises to help her in her plan to disguise herself as a young man and become one of Orsino's servants.

1.3: In Olivia's house, her uncle, Sir Toby Belch, introduces his friend, the foolish Sir Andrew Aguecheek, to Olivia's gentlewoman, Maria, whose wit proves too sharp for him. Sir Andrew has been invited to the house by Sir Toby so that he can woo Olivia, and despite his failure so far, he agrees to stay a month longer.

1.4: After only three days, Viola (now disguised and calling herself Cesario) has made a real impression on Orsino, who uses 'him' to take love-messages to Olivia. Viola obliges loyally, despite having fallen in love with Orsino.

1.5: Maria warns Feste, Olivia's fool, that he will be in trouble for staying away for so long. He succeeds in softening Olivia with his cleverness with words, but is clearly disliked by Olivia's steward, Malvolio, who insults him for his alleged lack of wit. A drunken Sir Toby enters to announce that there is someone at the gate. Showing great determination, Viola makes her way in and charms Olivia so much with her words of love on Orsino's behalf that Olivia falls in love with this good-looking and eloquent boy. In order to see Cesario again, Olivia pretends that he had left a ring and sends Malvolio after Cesario to return it.

Act 2

2.1: Viola's brother Sebastian arrives along the coast. Although Sebastian wants to journey on alone, the captain who has assisted him, Antonio, cannot resist following him, because of the great love that he feels for the boy.

2.2: Malvolio catches up with Viola and tries to return the ring. Viola realises that Olivia has fallen in love with her.

2.3: In the middle of the night, Sir Toby and Sir Andrew are joined by Feste in a drinking session. Maria arrives to advise them to keep the noise down, but, in the middle of a raucous song, Malvolio enters and rebukes them for their unruly behaviour, threatening to report Maria to her mistress. As Malvolio leaves, Maria outlines a plot which will enable them to take revenge on him: she will forge a love-letter addressed to him in Olivia's handwriting and drop it where he will find it.

2.4: Still emotional about his love for Olivia, Orsino asks for Feste, who sings a sad song about love and death. Orsino and Cesario (Viola) discuss the different ways in which men and woman react to love, and, in a story about her 'sister', Viola actually recounts her own love for Orsino.

2.5: In Olivia's garden, Sir Toby, Sir Andrew and a servant called Fabian hide behind a box-hedge as Malvolio enters, talking to himself about his ambitions to be Count Malvolio, marrying Olivia and using his new-found power against Sir Toby. He finds the letter and, after some puzzlement, realises that it is aimed at him. Ecstatically he leaves, determined to appear before Olivia wearing yellow, cross-gartered stockings and smiling, as the letter has instructed.

Act 3

3.1: Paying another visit to Olivia, Viola encounters Feste and learns about the nature of his fooling. She meets Olivia, who declares her love and asks Cesario to return the following day.

3.2: Having seen the welcome that Olivia gave to Cesario, Sir Andrew declares that he will leave, as he plainly doesn't stand a chance of marrying Olivia. To get him to stay, Sir Toby and Fabian persuade him that he can impress Olivia by a show of bravery and he goes off to write a letter challenging Cesario to a duel, leaving his friends greatly amused at the prospect of the cowardly Sir Andrew fighting the equally timid Cesario. At this point Maria enters to report that Malvolio is about to approach Olivia in yellow stockings, and they all run off to witness the outcome.

3.3: Antonio explains to Sebastian that, having reached the town, it will not be safe for him to accompany his friend any further, as he is a wanted man in Illyria (because of a dispute following a sea battle some years before). He gives Sebastian his money in case he needs any and they agree to meet later at the inn.

3.4: When Malvolio approaches Olivia, she becomes convinced that he is deranged, as this usually sober man is dressed in cross-gartered yellow stockings, smiles constantly and is over-familiar with her. Olivia of course fails to recognise any of the phrases he quotes from the forged letter and leaves, giving orders for her servants to look after her steward, who is plainly unwell. Sir Toby, Maria and Fabian then taunt Malvolio, pretending that he is mad and advising him to reject the devil that possesses him. They plan to have him locked up and bound in a darkened room.

Sir Andrew enters with his challenge. It is, of course, laughable and Sir Toby resolves privately that he will issue the challenge orally instead. As Viola takes her leave of Olivia, she is intercepted by Sir Toby who warns her of the violent fencer waiting to fight with her at the end of the garden. Sir Toby then moves from Viola to Sir Andrew, convincing each one that the other is a demon, but manages to bring the two together, despite their terror. The comic duel has hardly begun when it is interrupted by Antonio, who rushes in to protect – as he thinks – Sebastian. But he is spotted and arrested by two of Orsino's officers and forced to ask for his money back. Viola, of course, does not understand what he is talking about, but, after he is taken off, angry and bitter at being refused by the boy he had loved and supported, it dawns on Viola that, as he had called her Sebastian, her brother must still be alive.

Having watched the scene, Sir Toby persuades Sir Andrew that he has nothing to fear from Cesario and Sir Andrew goes off vowing to fight him.

Act 4

4.1: Just as Sebastian is becoming really irritated by Feste's insistence that he knows him (Feste, of course, thinks he is Cesario), in comes Sir Andrew and hits him. When Sebastian retaliates, Sir Toby joins in on Sir Andrew's side, but the fight is interrupted by Olivia, who (like the others, mistaking Sebastian for Cesario) speaks sternly to Sir Toby and then offers help and advice to Sebastian, who happily goes off with her, hardly able to believe his luck.

4.2: Feste disguises himself with a beard and gown as Sir Topas the priest and goes to taunt 'Malvolio the lunatic', who is by now desperate, having been confined in darkness for some time. Feste cleverly twists everything that Malvolio says, to prove that he is mad, but Sir Toby suggests that it is time for the game to end, as Olivia is angry with him. Speaking to him this time in his own voice, Feste agrees to fetch writing materials so that Malvolio can send a message to Olivia.

4.3: Sebastian is in a daze, wondering whether either he or Olivia is mad, and worrying about what has become of Antonio; but when Olivia enters with a priest, he happily agrees to marry her in secret.

Act 5

5.1: Feste refuses to let Fabian see Malvolio's letter and, when Viola and Orsino enter, manages to beg some money off the Duke. Orsino recognises Antonio when he is brought in under arrest and Viola explains that this is the stranger who stepped in to help her when she was fighting the duel. Thinking that he is looking at Sebastian, Antonio describes how he has looked after this ungrateful boy for three months, and is dumbfounded when Orsino confirms that the 'boy' has been with him for the whole of that period. When Olivia enters and rejects Orsino's offers of love yet again, Orsino turns to leave, but is stopped in his tracks by Olivia's naming of Cesario as her husband, and is bitterly angry at Cesario's apparent betrayal in having secretly wooed Olivia for himself. No sooner has the priest confirmed that Olivia and Cesario are married, than Sir Toby and Sir Andrew enter, bleeding from fights they have just had with 'Cesario' (in fact, Sebastian), who, as far as they can see, is standing next to Orsino. At this point Sebastian himself enters and assumes that Olivia is looking at him strangely because she is upset that he has wounded her uncle. As the others stand in silent amazement, Sebastian greets Antonio, relieved to see him again. Then Sebastian sees Viola and cannot believe his eyes. They confirm to each other that they are, in fact, brother and sister, and Sebastian explains to Olivia what has happened.

Realising that Cesario is in fact a woman who has served him faithfully, Orsino offers her his hand. Viola explains that her women's clothes are in the possession of the Captain, who has been arrested for some reason on Malvolio's instructions, and this reminds Olivia that her steward has become deranged. She asks Feste to read the letter that Malvolio has written, but, as he delivers it in a madman's voice, she tells Fabian to read it out instead. It is clearly not a madman's letter, and, when Malvolio enters, he accuses Olivia of treating him unjustly. When Olivia sees the letter that he has kept with him in his imprisonment, she recognises Maria's handwriting immediately. Fabian explains how the plot against Malvolio was carried out and reports that, as a reward for her cleverness, Sir Toby has married Maria. Feste taunts Malvolio by reminding him of the words in the forged letter and Malvolio leaves, threatening revenge. Orsino orders someone to follow Malvolio and pacify him and then announces his coming marriage to Viola. Feste ends the play with a bitter-sweet song about life.

Study skills: titles and quotations

Referring to titles

When you are writing an essay, you will often need to refer to the title of the play. There are two main ways of doing this:

- If you are handwriting your essay, the title of the play should be underlined: <u>Twelfth Night</u>.
- If you are word-processing your essay, the play title should be in italics: *Twelfth Night*.

The same rules apply to titles of all plays and other long works including novels and non-fiction, such as: *Animal Farm* and *The Diary of Anne Frank*. The titles of poems or short stories are placed inside single inverted commas; for example: 'Timothy Winters' and 'A Sound of Thunder'.

Note that the first word in a title and all the main words will have capital (or 'upper case') letters, while the less important words (such as conjunctions, prepositions and articles) will usually begin with lower case letters; for example: *The Taming of the Shrew* or *Antony and Cleopatra*.

Using quotations

Quotations show that you know the play in detail and are able to produce evidence from the script to back up your ideas and opinions. It is usually a good idea to keep quotations as short as you can (and this especially applies to exams, where it is a waste of time copying chunks out of the script).

Using long quotations

There are a number of things you should do if you want to use a quotation of more than a few words:

1. Make your point. —— **The importance of music is established right at the beginning of the play:** —————— 2. A colon introduces the quotation.

3. Leave a line. ——————

4. Indent the quotation. —— **If music be the food of love, play on;** —— 5. No quotation marks.

6. Keep the same line-divisions as the script. —— **Give me excess of it ...**

7. Three dots show that the quotations is incomplete.

8. Continue with a follow-up point, perhaps commenting on the quotation itself. —— **Orsino's words introduce not only the ...**

Using brief quotations

Brief quotations are usually easier to use, take less time to write out and are much more effective in showing how familiar you are with the play. Embed them in the sentence like this:

- When, in the first line of the play, Orsino calls music 'the food of love', it is clear that . . .
- It is largely because he is 'sick of self-love' that Malvolio is so easy to trick . . .
- Although Viola soon recognises that disguise is 'a wickedness', she has no choice but to . . .

If you are asked to state where the quotation comes from, use this simple form of reference:

- Toby's description of Maria as 'the youngest wren of nine' (3.2.65) is an indication that . . .

In some editions this is written partly in Roman numerals – upper case for the Act and lower case for the scene; for example: (III.ii.65), or (III.2.65).

William Shakespeare and *Twelfth Night*

The complete title of this play, as it appeared in the First Folio is actually *Twelfth Night or What You Will*. It is not known exactly when it was written, but a law student, John Manningham, recorded in his diary that he had seen a performance of it in 1602. This is how it fits into Shakespeare's career and the times in which he lived.

Shakespeare's life and career

No one is absolutely sure when he wrote each play.

1564   Born in Stratford-upon-Avon, first son of John and Mary Shakespeare.

1582   Marries Anne Hathaway from the nearby village of Shottery. She is eight years older and expecting their first child.

1583   Daughter Susanna born.

1585   Twin son and daughter, Hamnet and Judith, born.

Some time before 1592 Shakespeare arrives in London, becomes an actor and writes poems and plays. Several plays are performed, probably including the three parts of *Henry VI*. Another writer, Robert Greene, writes about 'Shake-scene', the 'upstart crow' who has clearly become a popular playwright.

By March 1595 he is a shareholder with the Lord Chamberlain's Men (see page 206) and has probably written *Richard III*, *Comedy of Errors*, *Titus Andronicus*, *Taming of the Shrew*, *Two Gentlemen of Verona*, *Love's Labours Lost*, *Romeo and Juliet*, *Richard II* and *A Midsummer Night's Dream* (as well as contributing to plays by other writers and writing the poems 'Venus and Adonis' and 'The Rape of Lucrece').

1596   Hamnet dies, aged 11.
1597   Buys New Place, one of the finest houses in Stratford.
1599   Globe theatre opens on Bankside.

By 1599: *King John, Merchant of Venice*, the two parts of *Henry IV, Merry Wives of Windsor, Much Ado About Nothing, Julius Caesar* and *Henry V* (as well as the Sonnets).

1603   King James I grants the Lord Chamberlain's Men a Royal Patent and they become the King's Men (page 206).

By 1608: *As You Like It, Hamlet, Twelfth Night, Troilus and Cressida, All's Well That Ends Well, Measure for Measure, Othello, Macbeth, King Lear, Antony and Cleopatra, Pericles, Coriolanus* and *Timon of Athens.*

1608   The King's Men begin performing plays in the indoor Blackfriars theatre (page 205).

By 1613: *Cymbeline, The Winter's Tale, The Tempest, Henry VIII, Two Noble Kinsmen* (the last two probably with John Fletcher).

1613   Globe theatre destroyed by fire.
1614   The rebuilt Globe theatre opens.
1616   Dies, 23 April, and is buried in Holy Trinity Church, Stratford.
1623   Publication of the First Folio (page 207).

Shakespeare's times

1558   Elizabeth I becomes queen.
1565   The sailor John Hawkins introduces sweet potatoes and tobacco into England.
1567   Mary Queen of Scots is forced to abdicate in favour of her year-old son, James VI.
1567   The first-known playhouse in London, the Red Lion, is built.
1568   Mary escapes to England and is imprisoned by Elizabeth.
1572   Francis Drake attacks Spanish ports in the Americas.
1576   James Burbage opens the Theatre in London.
1580   Francis Drake returns from the first English circumnavigation of the world.
1582   Pope Gregory reforms the Christian calendar.
1587   Mary Queen of Scots executed for a treasonous plot against Elizabeth; Drake destroys two dozen Spanish ships at Cadiz and war breaks out with Spain.
1588   Philip II of Spain's Armada is defeated by the English fleet.
1593   Plague kills 11,000 Londoners.

1593   Playwright Christopher Marlowe killed in a pub brawl.
1595   The Earl of Tyrone leads a new rebellion in Ireland.
1596   Tomatoes introduced into England; John Harington invents the water-closet (the ancestor of the modern lavatory).
1599   The Earl of Essex concludes a truce with Tyrone, returns home and is arrested.
1601   Essex is tried and executed for treasonous plots against Elizabeth.
1603   Elizabeth I dies and is succeeded by James VI of Scotland as James I of England.
1603   Sir Walter Raleigh is jailed for plotting against James.
1604   James is proclaimed 'King of Great Britain, France and Ireland'; new Church rules cause 300 Puritan clergy to resign.
1605   Gunpowder Plot uncovered.
1607   First permanent English settlement in America at Jamestown, Virginia.
1610   Galileo looks at the stars through a telescope; tea is introduced into Europe.
1611   The Authorised Version of the Bible published.
1618   Raleigh executed; physician William Harvey announces discovery of blood circulation.
1620   Pilgrim Fathers sail from Plymouth to colonise America.
1625   James I dies and is succeeded by Charles I.

Index of activities